IDEAS FOR ASSEMBLIES

KS 1

Pl to 3

AUTHOR
Georgie Beasley

DESIGNER
Rachael Hammond

EDITOR
Kate Pearce

ILLUSTRATIONS
Mike Phillips

ASSISTANT EDITOR
Roanne Davis

COVER ARTWORK
Ian Murray

SERIES DESIGNER
Anna Oliwa

Text © 2000 Georgie Beasley
© 2000 Scholastic Ltd

Designed using Adobe Pagemaker
Published by Scholastic Ltd, Villiers House, Clarendon
Avenue, Leamington Spa, Warwickshire CV32 5PR
Printed by Bell & Bain Ltd, Glasgow

67890 456789

British Library Cataloguing-in-Publication Data
A catalogue record for this book is available from the
British Library.

ISBN 0-439-01776-9

372. 840 44
409376

ACKNOWLEDGEMENTS
JILL JESSON FOR THE USE OF 'NEW
YEAR RESOLUTION' FROM *SCHOLASTIC
COLLECTIONS: ASSEMBLIES*. COMPILED BY
IAN ADDIS AND SUE SPOONER © 1994,
Jill Jesson (1994, Scholastic
Publications Ltd.).

Donation

Contents

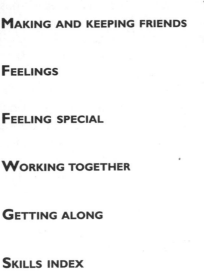

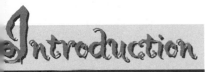

Introduction

The assemblies in this book are planned to deal with a number of issues which young children find difficult but need to learn how to handle. They contribute to children's developing understanding of what is acceptable and unacceptable behaviour by allowing them to consider the impact of their actions on others. The assemblies revisit and foster the values of fairness, honesty, truth and politeness. Pupils are encouraged to consider their role in developing and keeping friends, caring for theirs' and others' belongings, respecting and caring for the environment, helping one another and consideration of others' feelings. The issues of race, gender and bullying are also covered throughout. The children are encouraged to develop an increasing self-awareness through which their self-esteem and self-worth are increased. While there are appropriate links made to the Bible and other faiths, the content of the assemblies is deliberately not directly taken from the Bible or other faiths except for the story of Joseph and the Jewish celebration of Hannukah. There are many books on Festival and Bible stories and they can therefore be used for additional assemblies if you wish.

ABOUT THIS BOOK

The book is organized into six sections each containing four or five interrelated assemblies, which deal with issues on a related theme. The first section deals with the Created World and our responsibilities to care for it. The second set of assemblies are about the way we make and keep friends; something that very young children often find difficult to do. The third is about feelings and how to handle the way we feel when things are fine and when things go wrong. The fourth is linked to raising self-esteem by considering the fact that we are all special, that we have our own special qualities and that everyone's contribution is important and valuable. The final two sections of assemblies deal with the important issues of working together and getting along. The need to consider the feelings of others and to develop empathy is stressed in these chapters. Multi-faith links are also made and these should be considered in the light of your school's context.

Each assembly is organized into six headings.

■ The learning objective is specific and focused and can easily be matched to any LEA Agreed Syllabus. It is linked very closely to the content of the assembly.

■ The resources needed for each assembly are given, including a reference to the photocopiable sheet and its use, and the need for additional adult support and contribution where necessary. Although specific music has not been included, it is recommended that appropriate music is used to support reflection and consideration of moods and feelings. Guidance is given on the most appropriate organization needed to support effectively the delivery of the assembly. A number of assemblies can be carried out as class assemblies presented to the whole school and usually contain some element of drama, while others are specifically tailored to whole-school or key-stage groups, and some are best presented to smaller class-sized groups. These are usually the ones where it is desirable for all children to have an opportunity to consider and contribute to the difficult issues and themes presented.

■ Specific cross-curricular links have been included and cover many curriculum subjects including literacy and numeracy, personal and social education, and spiritual, moral, social and cultural development. Reference has also been made to the QCA schemes of work where appropriate. Particular reference is given to spiritual development in all assemblies when opportunities for reflection and the collective act of worship are included.

■ The 'What to do' section gives step-by-step instructions on how to deliver the assembly. It includes the poems, stories, drama, discussion and debate which form the main part of the content. Guidance on making displays, writing rules and prayers and the use of teaching aids is given. This section also gives ideas for prayers and hymns to fulfil the statutory requirement for a collective act of worship, although it is recommended that these are tailored to individual school's needs and cultural make-up. Guidance is also given on how to integrate the element of reflection into the assembly. Young children do not reflect naturally, therefore guidance is included in this section on how you can contribute to the quality of this assembly by questioning and leading the children's thoughts through the ideas presented. Guidance is also offered on how to organize the content and activities, and suggested questions are given to develop the children's opinions, encourage their ideas and make the assembly interactive.

■ Suggestions for differentiation include opportunities to extend the activities with the older or more able children while also offering suggestions for support to reinforce the learning objective for those children who need it.

■ The 'Now or later' section contains ideas which can be used to develop or substitute some of the content of the assembly to better match the needs of the children in your school. Included in this section is a reference to stories from the Bible and some links to stories and poems from other faiths. These contribute in some way to the children's spiritual development by asking them to gain an understanding and respect for their own and others' beliefs. This section also gives follow-up suggestions linked to the theme of the assembly, which can be carried out in the classroom or developed into an additional assembly.

The skill reference sheet at the back of the book is useful for assessment, and for ensuring that the children are following a comprehensive, progressive and continuous programme to develop their learning needs.

Finally, there are a set of useful photocopiable sheets included at the end of each section which include the stories, poems, prayers and teaching aids needed to make this book a one stop shop for assemblies.

Section 1   OUR WONDERFUL WORLD

The assemblies in this section focus on children learning to:
- develop the knowledge that many people believe in a god and some use a different name for God
- recognize that the Bible is a special book used by Christians
- reflect on their own behaviour and actions and to be aware that these impact upon others and the environment
- develop consideration for the environment
- understand that there are different characteristics of simple prayers
- listen to and consider stories about the celebrations of different faiths.

IN THE BEGINNING

RESOURCES AND ORGANIZATION

You will need: a set of seven pictures depicting the Creation story from the Old Testament (enlarged copies of the pictures on photocopiable page 12 will suffice, although you will need to draw your own picture for the seventh day – this has not been included on the photocopiable sheet); copies of photocopiable page 12, enlarged if required and prepared for use with an overhead projector if one is available; a display board; the Creation story from the Bible, Genesis chapter 1, verses 1-27, or a children's version of the story; a Bible; crayons, scissors and glue; a soft piece of music and cassette/CD player (optional).

This could be organized as a whole school assembly, or as a class assembly presented to the school. Each group of children could hold up large paintings of the Creation story as the story is told.

WHAT TO DO

Make sure the children are sitting so that they can easily see the display board onto which you intend to display the pictures. Begin the assembly by singing the hymn 'He's Got the Whole World in His Hands' from *Someone's Singing, Lord* (A&C Black).

Show the children the Bible and explain that it is a special book which Christians believe tells the stories about God and Jesus. Tell the children that they are going to hear the first story in the Bible which tells how God created the world. Explain that it is a story which Christians believe. Turn to the page in the Bible and read the first sentence of Genesis, chapter 1. Either read the Creation story to the children or tell the story in your own words, using the pictures as prompt sheets. When you have finished, pin the pictures to the display board in the wrong sequential order. Talk to the children about the story and what they can see in the pictures. Explain that the

OBJECTIVE
To learn that Christians believe in God and that the Bible is a special book which says that He created the world.

CROSS-CURRICULAR LINKS
ENGLISH
This activity links well with literacy when used as a sequencing task.

RE
Older or more able children could listen to and consider creation stories from other faiths.

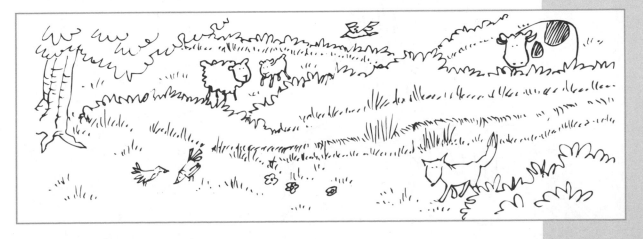

pictures are in the wrong order and that together you are going to reorder them correctly according to what God created first, second, and so on. Ask the children if they can remember what God made first. Say something like: *Yes, that's right. God made the heavens and the Earth first. Did He like what He saw?* Continue in this way until you have ordered all the pictures correctly. Reiterate that this story comes from the Bible (hold it up again to show the children) and is believed by Christians.

Emphasize that other faiths have similar, but not the same, beliefs.

Ask the children to think quietly about the world that they live in while you mention things like the quiet of the morning, the white of the snow, the colours of the flowers, and so on. You may wish to play a quiet piece of music in the background at this point to sustain the children's thoughts. After a few moments, say the prayer, opposite.

> Thank you God for the beautiful Earth, the skies and the heavens; for the sun and stars and moon.
> Thank you for the water; for the seas, rivers, lakes and streams.
> Thank you for the plants; for the trees and flowers and crops.
> Thank you for the landscapes; for the mountains, hills and plains; for the fields, meadows and gardens.
> We give thanks for the creatures and peoples of the world.
> Help us to care for them all while we are living here on Earth.
> Amen.

SUGGESTIONS FOR DIFFERENTIATION

To reinforce the learning objective, on return to the classroom, give each child a copy of photocopiable page 12 and explain that they are going to repeat the sequencing activity. If you wish, they can colour the pictures before cutting them out and sticking them into a book or onto paper in the correct order. Remind them that they will need to draw their own picture for the seventh day and write a simple sentence beneath each picture to retell the story of the Creation. Once you are sure the majority of children understand the task, return to the support group and talk to them as you complete the task together. Keep an eye on the other groups at opportune moments.

Talk to the older or more able children about the Bible. Explain that the Bible is divided into two Testaments or volumes, just as the set of encyclopaedia in the library is organized into volumes. Tell them that the Old Testament tells stories about peoples, places and times before Jesus was born, while the New Testament tells about his life and the period after He died.

NOW OR LATER

■ Talk to the children about the Hindu deities and Muslims calling God Allah.

■ Read the children other creation stories, both religious and non-religious. Include the story of the Buddha creating the first man – Manu.

■ Use prayers from a variety of faiths in your assemblies, to reinforce the knowledge that most major religions believe that there is only one god.

■ Explain that the creation story is also found in the Jewish Torah.

ALL THINGS BRIGHT AND BEAUTIFUL

RESOURCES AND ORGANIZATION

Plan a display depicting the items from the first and last verse and the chorus of the hymn 'All Things Bright and Beautiful'. Cover a display board with pale blue and green backing paper to depict the sky and the grass. Collect pictures of the sun, flowers, birds, animals, trees, fruit, and so on. You will also need a stapler and staples.

This is equally successful as a whole-school, key-stage or class assembly. You will need sufficient space to allow the children to come out to attach the pictures to the display. Organize additional adult support to help younger children staple the items.

WHAT TO DO

Sit the children around the display board and teach them the verses and chorus of 'All Things Bright and Beautiful' if they do not already know the hymn.

Show the children the pictures you have gathered and explain that you are going to create a display together showing the wonderful world that God has made and all the beautiful things in it. Sing the chorus and first verse again, holding up the pictures of flowers, animals, trees, fruits, birds and the sun. After the children have finished singing, invite a small group of children to help you staple the pictures to the display, discussing and talking about the pictures as you do so.

Sing the first verse and chorus through twice again if you wish. When you have completed this part of the assembly, sing the final verse together. Spend a short time reflecting on the meaning of this verse. What do the children think they should do with their eyes and lips? Is this verse saying we should only enjoy the world? Do we have a responsibility to look after it? What would happen if we didn't look after our world? Would we be wise if we didn't? How long would the world stay bright, beautiful and wonderful? Can the children name something in the display which is bright/beautiful/wise/wonderful? Can they give reasons for their choices? Emphasize how thankful we are for our wonderful world, and the need to care for it.

Say the traditional prayer, below.

> Father, we thank Thee for the night
> And for the pleasant morning light,
> For rest and food and loving care,
> And all that makes the world so fair.
> Help us to do the things we should.
> To be to others kind and good,
> In all we do, in all we say,
> To grow more loving every day.
> Amen.

Finally, bring the assembly to a close by singing 'Stand Up, Clap Hands, Shout Thank You Lord' from *Someone's Singing, Lord* (A&C Black).

Before the children leave, tell them that the display will be complete when their eyes and lips have been added. Explain that when they return to their classroom, you want them to draw pictures of themselves to add to the display. When these are finished, staple the portraits around the edge of the display to form a border and label it with appropriate words including 'bright', 'beautiful', 'wonderful' and 'wise'.

SUGGESTIONS FOR DIFFERENTIATION

Develop the assembly over a number of days. Start at the beginning of the week by discussing the creatures great and small; Tuesday discuss the flowers and the birds; Wednesday look at landscape features; Thursday discuss the weather; and on Friday look at the five senses we have to appreciate the world in which we live.

NOW OR LATER

■ Read the story of Holi and create a dance to depict the story.
■ Include the Hindu prayer 'The Gayatri Mantra' in your assemblies and display a copy next to your display.

> **The Gayatri Mantra**
> Oh God, Creator and Life-Giver of the Universe;
> Everywhere and in all things,
> We meditate on your Splendour and Divine Light
> And pray for purity of mind and knowledge of the Truth.

OBJECTIVE
To reinforce the children's understanding that Christians believe that the world was made by God and that they should give thanks.

CROSS-CURRICULAR LINKS

ART AND DESIGN
The children can consider portraits by famous artists as part of an art appreciation lesson. Talk about how they have created the person's features.

ENGLISH
As a group activity, look up the meanings of some of the words used in the assembly in the dictionary, for example 'wonderful', 'beautiful', 'bright' and 'wise'.

SCIENCE
Carry out a survey of all the plant and animal life around the school.

THANK YOU FOR THE WORLD

OBJECTIVE
To learn that when we pray we are talking and listening to God.

CROSS-CURRICULAR LINKS
RE
Children can use the writing frame on photocopiable page 13 to write their own thank-you prayers. Display these around an enlarged copy of the communal prayer.

RESOURCES AND ORGANIZATION
You will need: a flip chart; overhead projector (optional); an enlarged copy of the writing frame on photocopiable page 13; a thick, dark-coloured felt-tipped pen; a calm piece of music and cassette/CD player (optional). Find a few prayers which say thank you to God or use the examples given below, and copy these onto large sheets of paper or overhead projector transparencies.

This assembly can be organized as a whole-school, key-stage or class assembly.

WHAT TO DO
When the children are settled, explain that together you are going to write a thank-you prayer thanking God for the wonderful world he has made. Ask the children to tell you about all the wonderful things in the world and jot their suggestions on the flip chart. Display the list where it can be seen for easy reference.

Next, talk to the children about how God is addressed. Refer to prayers that the children already know, for example 'The Lord's Prayer' and 'Thank You for the World', or one from their own religion, and spend a few moments talking and thinking about the things that we pray about. Include things such as helping us to remember the proper way to behave, treating others with kindness and respect, guiding us to be good, asking for forgiveness when we do wrong. Explain that today you are going to write a thank-you prayer together, and that you want to choose from the many ways that God is addressed when we say thank you. Read the beginnings of a few thank-you prayers to the children and talk about the beginnings with them. See the example, left. (These examples can be copied and used on an overhead projector or can be jotted down on another piece of paper and displayed alongside the first sheet.)

- ■ We thank thee Lord for this wonderful world.
- ■ Lord Jesus who is in Heaven, thank you for…
- ■ Thank you God for all the plants and the creatures who live in our world.
- ■ Help us to look after our world.
- ■ Dear God, thank you for this wonderful world.
- ■ For all the flowers and trees in the world, thank you Lord.
- ■ Our Father who is in Heaven, thank you for the world.
- ■ We pray for all the living things in the world.
- ■ Father we thank you for the plants and creatures, for the…

Now ask the children to consider the ideas. Which one do they want to use to start their prayer? Record the chosen beginning on your enlarged copy of the writing frame on photocopiable page 13.

Next, ask the children which of their ideas they would like to include in their prayer. Choose several from the first sheet of paper and link the ideas so that they are not merely a list of unrelated thoughts. When you have recorded the ideas, discuss with the children how you are going to finish the prayer. Again, use a few chosen examples for ideas if you wish. Select an ending and add this to your prayer.

Listen to a calm and peaceful piece of music and reflect upon the things that have been included in the prayer. Talk quietly to the children about things they may have omitted. Say something like: *Let us also consider….* Finally, say the prayer together and sing the hymn 'Stand Up, Clap Hands, Shout Thank You Lord' or 'He Gave Me Eyes' from *Someone's Singing, Lord* (A&C Black) to bring the assembly to a close.

SUGGESTIONS FOR DIFFERENTIATION
Work in small groups to discuss the things that have been included in the prayer. Encourage the more able children to consider including in the prayer issues such as people's characteristics, taking care of our environment and the contribution we have to make as people in order to make the world a better place in which to live.

NOW OR LATER
- ■ Display the suggestion sheet for the children to add their ideas during the week.
- ■ Refer to the different hand positions used by Muslims and Rastafarians during prayer.

■ Organize an activity for children to write their own prayers and use some of them in later assemblies when you consider the natural world.
■ Explain that the Sikh Golden Temple at Amritsar has doors facing in four directions because God is everywhere.
■ Read the story of Adam and Eve in the Garden of Eden (Genesis 2. 4–23).
■ Refer to the Sikhs' prayer and the Hindus ringing of a bell on entry to a place of worship. The ringing of the bell announces that the person is there. It informs the gods and asks them to be aware of the person.

A FESTIVAL OF LIGHT

RESOURCES AND ORGANIZATION

You will need: the story of Hanukkah; a picture of a synagogue; a menorah or a picture of one. All these can be found on photocopiable pages 14 to 16.

This assembly is effective as a class assembly presented to the school, a whole-school or key-stage assembly.

WHAT TO DO

Settle the children and show them the picture of the synagogue on photocopiable page 14 or any others you have found. Tell them that this is the place where Jewish people go to worship God. Explain that every year, usually in November or December, Jewish people celebrate the eight-day festival of Hanukkah in which they remember a very special time when a family of Jews, called the Macabees, became victorious over the Syrians.

Read the children the story of Hanukkah on photocopiable page 15. (Photocopiable page 16 contains a picture of a menorah which you can show at the appropriate part of the story if you have been unable to obtain an actual one.) When you have finished the story, talk to the children about the faith and courage of the Jewish people. How do they think the people felt when they went into battle? Do they think the same outcome could have been achieved in a less violent way? Explain to the children that the Jewish people believe that the burning of the oil for eight days was a miracle, a special sign sent by God.

Show the children the menorah, or the picture, and point out the candles. The first candle is lit on the first day, the second on the second day, and so on until all the candles have been lit. (The ninth candle in the centre is the one used to light the other eight.) Talk to the children about some of the special food that Jewish people eat at this time to give thanks to God, such as cheese, and potato latkes, a kind of potato pancake cooked in oil. Finish with a short period of reflection while the children think about how the Jewish people must have felt when they were not allowed to pray to God, and were forced to pray to another, and then how their feelings must have changed when they could. Say the prayer opposite for the children to repeat.

Finish the assembly by singing 'Give Me Oil In My Lamp' from *Come and Praise* (BBC publications).

> Our God in heaven
> Thank you for keeping us safe.
> Thank you for the freedom
> to pray to the God that we choose.
> Amen.

OBJECTIVE
To learn that Jews celebrate the festival of light through Hanukkah.

CROSS-CURRICULAR LINKS
SCIENCE
Talk to the children about what gives us light. Make a list of all the natural and man-made light sources that they think of.

GEOGRAPHY
Look at a large map of the Middle East and find Syria and Israel.

SUGGESTIONS FOR DIFFERENTIATION

Conduct the story as a play. You will need to choose children to play Judas Maccabeus and his army, a group of Jewish people who go to the temple to pray, Antiochus and his soldiers, and the small boy. Some additional explanation of the way people used to live may be necessary. Make a copy of photocopiable page 15 for a narrator to read as the children act out the story.

NOW OR LATER

■ Make potato pancakes for the children to share.
■ Read some of the miracles performed by Jesus and talk to the children about the concept of miracles.
■ Read the story of Divali and repeat the assembly for this festival, making Divali lamps from clay.
■ Talk to the children about the Christian belief that Jesus is the light of the world, and the meaning of Advent.
■ Make Christingles with the children.

LET'S CELEBRATE

OBJECTIVE

To learn that every year we have another opportunity to put things right by making New Year's Resolutions.

CROSS-CURRICULAR LINKS

DESIGN AND TECHNOLOGY
■ The children could design a poster to remind people how to look after the environment. Display these in a prominent position for all parents and carers to see as well as the children.
■ Use recyclable materials to make a model of a robot.

PSHE

Talk to the children about not picking up litter and rubbish unless an adult says it is safe to do so.

RESOURCES AND ORGANIZATION

You will need: a collection of old newspapers, empty aluminium cans, empty glass bottles, discarded wrapping paper, tin foil, stamps, various bits of litter and a waste-paper bin. These should all be displayed on a table in a space where the children can see them easily. You will also need a bowl of warm water, soap and a towel.

This assembly works well as the first assembly to the whole school in the new year, although it could be successful at other times if set within a different context such as 'Turning over a new leaf', 'Starting a new term afresh' or 'It's never too late to start again'.

WHAT TO DO

Begin the assembly by singing the hymn 'Milk Bottle Tops and Paper Bags' from *Someone's Singing, Lord* (A&C Black).

Draw the children's attention to the items on display and talk to them about your collection. Ask them to tell you what they can see. Explain that you have brought in these items to help you explain your New Year's Resolution – you have decided to help look after the environment by recycling as many things as possible.

Show the children the rubbish you have in your collection and ask them what would happen if we all decided to drop our rubbish on the floor. If you wish, tell them a short story about seeing someone casually dropping their chocolate wrapper in the street. Ask what that person could have done instead. After the discussion, place your litter collection in the bin. Remind the children at this point that they should not pick up rubbish themselves unless an adult says it is safe to do so. Tell them that you must now wash your hands even though the rubbish belongs to you.

Explain to the children that you would not necessarily throw all the things on the table in the bin. Some of the things can be used again, which would help to conserve the world's natural resources. Show the children a drink can and explain that it can be sent to a special place where it will be crushed with other cans of the same material and remade into a new can. Explain that glass bottles and jars can be recycled in the same way, for example jam jars, drinks bottles and sauce bottles.

In turn, show the children the other items you have and explain how they will be recycled for future use. At the end, wash your hands again, explaining why you are doing so to the children.

Now ask the children whether they have made any New Year's Resolutions. You will probably get the usual 'give up sweets and biscuits', but positively encourage those children who make suggestions such as 'helping someone who needs it every day', or 'tidying away my things without being asked'. Spend a few moments of quiet, reflecting on some of the things the children could promise to do, followed by the prayer 'New Year's Resolution' by Jill Jesson found in the *Scholastic Collections: Assemblies* book.

This year…
> I will act as if everything I say or do can make a difference

This year…
> I will do one thing to help at home every day

This year…
> I will say one kind, true thing to someone who needs my help every month,

This year…
> I will recycle everything I can throughout the year, so that…

This year…
> I will make a difference to the world.

When the children have returned to the classroom, explain that you want them to write down their New Year's Resolutions. If they have not already thought of a good resolution, explain that you want them to think of one now. They may draw a picture if they wish.

SUGGESTIONS FOR DIFFERENTIATION

Work with small groups of children in the classroom talking about New Year's Resolutions and the idea of recycling to help look after the world. Encourage them to include one idea for taking care of the environment in their New Year's Resolution list. Set up a display in each classroom to reinforce the message.

NOW OR LATER

■ Approach the local council for sponsorship to provide a colourful and topical litter bin for the school playground to encourage the children to deposit their litter. Invite the children to design a litter bin and send the design proposal to a local firm to ask their advice on whether its production is feasible.

■ Set up a recycling project or a school environment club where the children can collect and sort clean items for recycling.

■ Carry out a survey and plot where the local recycling points and litterbugs are in the environment on maps of the local area.

■ Learn about the Chinese and Jewish New Years and how these religions celebrate.

■ Talk about New Year in different religions and in different parts of the world, for example Divali, the Chinese New Year, Ganjitsu, Rastafarian New Year. Ganjitsu is the Japanese New Year. It is a family festival with decorations, processions and food. People wish each other good luck and health. The Ethiopian New Year takes place in September and is celebrated with dancing, drumming, singing and prayer.

In the beginning

■ Cut out the pictures and put them in the right order.

All things bright and beautiful

A synagogue

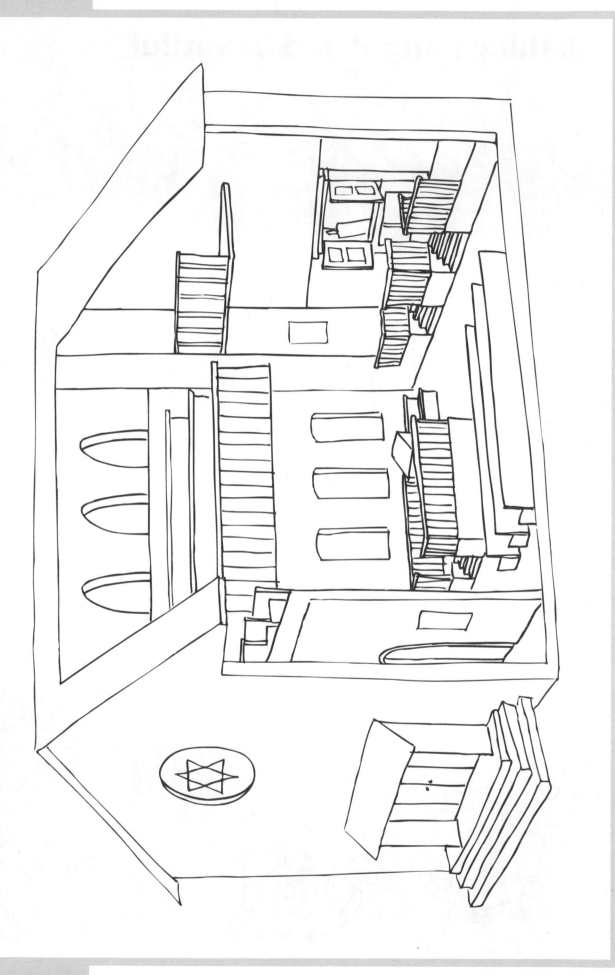

Hanukkah

Hanukkah (also spelt Chanukah or Hannukah) is the Jewish festival of light. It celebrates the time when a man called Judas Maccabeus won a battle against a king called Antiochus. This is the story that is told.

A long time ago the Jewish people lived in a land which is now called Israel. One day a very big army marched into Israel from a neighbouring country called Syria, led by a king called Antiochus. There was a very fierce battle and the Jewish people fought bravely, but the Syrians won the battle.

Now the Syrians were not very kind people. They told the Jewish people that they must do everything that Antiochus their king said. He said that they had to worship the Syrians' Gods and not the God that they believed in. They could not go to their own temple to worship their God and the Syrian soldiers stood guard to make sure that they did not. This made the Jewish people very unhappy. They did not want to worship these other Gods. They thought it was wrong to worship the Syrian Gods and if they refused, they were killed by the Syrian soldiers.

One day a shepherd called Judas Maccabeus said he would lead the Jewish people into battle. He gathered a very large army together and trained them to fight. He knew that the army was much smaller than the Syrian army but he was determined to win.

The day came when there was a great battle. Judas led his army into battle on a horse and Antiochus rode a huge elephant. When Judas and Antiochus met, everyone thought that Antiochus was safe on his elephant but Judas was very clever. In those days the animals wore armour to protect them. Judas struck the elephant in the right place underneath the armour. The elephant fell to the ground and Antiochus was killed when he fell off the animal. Judas and his army fought until they won the battle.

The Jewish army marched back to their town. They threw out all the statues of Gods that they had been made to worship and started to pray in their temple again. Everyone was very happy now that they could worship their own God again. The Jewish people came to the temple to pray and to give thanks to God. But there were no candles to burn. A small boy found one small oil lamp with enough oil to burn for one day. It would be eight days before any more oil would be ready. What were the people to do? It was part of their religion to burn a light whenever they prayed. How could they pray without burning a light? Still, they lit the lamp and prayed to God for delivering them from the Syrians. They thought it was better to burn the light for just one day than not to burn it at all.

The Jewish people were amazed when the lamp burned for eight days – long enough for more oil to be made. They thought this was a miracle and ever since that day they have held a celebration every year to remember the time when the oil lamp had burned for eight days instead of one so that they could pray to God.

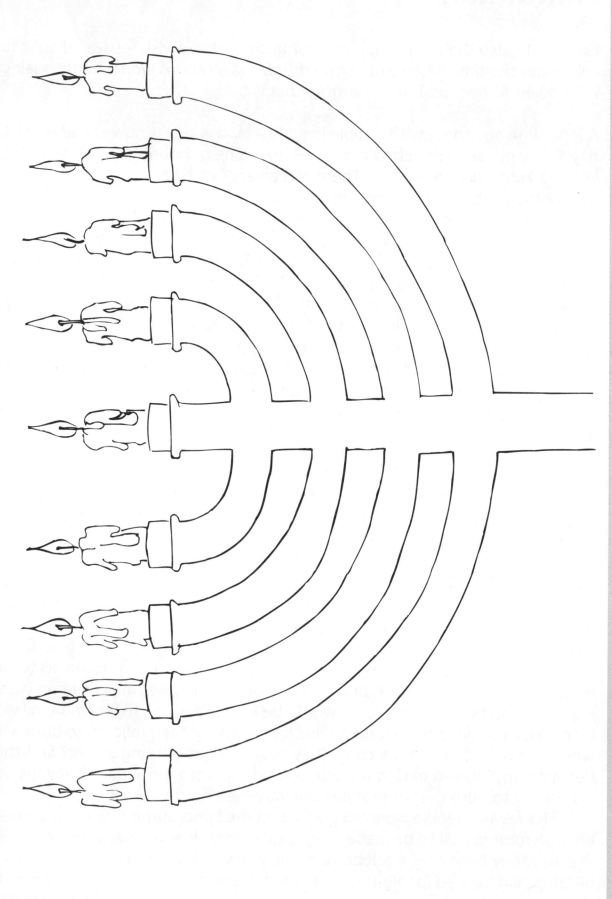

A menorah

The assemblies in this section focus on children learning to:
■ identify their role in establishing and keeping friendships
■ develop the moral values of caring, consideration, forgiveness, love, sharing and helpfulness
■ locate themes within faiths and practices of Christianity, Islam, Hinduism, Judaism, Sikhism and Buddhism
■ understand the feelings of others as well as their own
■ say why they should behave in a certain way.

FRIENDSHIP CAKE

RESOURCES AND ORGANIZATION

You will need: a table covered in a cloth; a see-through mixing bowl; a wooden spoon; 120g of soft margarine, two eggs, 120g of castor sugar, 120g of self-raising flour; transparent food bags sealed with ties.

This is equally successful as a whole-school or class assembly. Gather the children in a semicircle so that they can all see the cake mixture and can easily gain access to add their ingredient. Check for food allergies if you intend to share the cake with the children afterwards.

WHAT TO DO

Show the children the ingredients you have on the table and ask them what they are. Explain that you are going to make a very special friendship cake, a cake which, when given to a friend, will hopefully ensure that they stay your friend forever.

Mix the ingredients following a traditional recipe, explaining how important it is to mix the ingredients together well so as to make a good cake, which will grow and rise when cooked. As you are mixing, talk to the children about one of your own special friendships, explaining why it is so special – perhaps you have supported each other in a particular way, or visited a special place together. This will keep the children's thoughts focused on the learning intentions.

When the mixture is complete, look somewhat puzzled and say something like: *Well this is a bit of an ordinary cake. I'm sure my friends will like it, but will it keep us friends forever if we share a piece? Is there anything else I ought to put in the mixture to make it a special cake for keeping friends?*

OBJECTIVE

To learn that we all have a responsibility to our friends through being kind and considerate, sharing our games and toys, showing we care, helping each other and sometimes forgiving each other.

CROSS-CURRICULAR LINKS

DESIGN AND TECHNOLOGY
The children may wish to design and make their own recipe for a friendship cake.

PSHE

Children consider their behaviour and attitudes towards each other in the playground.

Pretend to look under the table or in your pocket for other ingredients. After a short time, pick up one of the transparent food bags, look at it carefully, open it and tip the 'contents' into the mixture, saying: *I've found some caring in this bag. I'll put it into the mixture and give it a good stir to mix it all together.*

Repeat this with another bag, naming a different value which will help to keep friends, such as love, helpfulness, consideration, sharing and forgiveness. When you think the children have understood the purpose of the cake mixture, invite them to come out and add their own 'ingredients' such as helping each other, sharing toys and games, playing together, or taking care of someone who is new or upset, for example. Stir these new 'ingredients' into the cake mixture. Emphasize again the importance of giving the mixture a good stir to blend in all of your ingredients for keeping friends.

Thank the children and explain that you will cook the cake and show it to them later in the day.

Ask the children to sit very still and to reflect quietly while you talk about the additional ingredients that have been added to the mixture. Say a short prayer to include the values that they have thought of, relating them to Christianity or another major religion.

> Dear God
> Thank you for all the people in the world.
> Let us learn to work together and play together,
> To help one another and show that we care.
> Help us to recognize other people's kindness and strength.
> Amen

Finish with an appropriate hymn, for example 'Jesus' Hands are Kind Hands' from *Someone's Singing, Lord* (A&C Black), before returning to the classroom. Share the baked cake with the children (making sure there is enough to go round).

SUGGESTIONS FOR DIFFERENTIATION

Repeat the activity in a classroom context to allow all the children an opportunity to add an extra ingredient and talk individually about the things they have added. Some children may continue to think of items throughout the week. Encourage them to contribute to a wall display showing their suggestions.

NOW OR LATER

■ Ask the children to write their own 'recipes' for a friendship cake and then make a display of the children's ideas. Staple a picture of a cake in the centre of the display and attach the children's recipes around the outside. Include bags or pots labelled with ingredients such as helpfulness, sharing, caring, consideration, forgiveness, taking turns and playing together.

■ Read the story from Luke chapters 5 and 6 in the New Testament about Jesus choosing his twelve disciples. Ask the children why they think Jesus chose the people He did. *Was it because they were important or ordinary people? Was it because they had lots of money? Was it because they were all good people to know?*

THANK YOU FOR MY FRIENDS

RESOURCES AND ORGANIZATION

You will need: squares of white paper measuring approximately 20cm × 20cm; crayons and felt-tipped pens in a variety of colours; a display board large enough to display the children's pictures in a patchwork pattern; card for labels; a stapler; an enlarged copy of the poem on photocopiable page 24, or for use on an OHP.

This works best as a class assembly and RE lesson, which will take approximately 45 minutes. If you decide to organize the activity as a school assembly, carry out the activity over two days and for your second assembly prepare your display board to include a few finished pictures already stapled into place. Organize the children so that they can all see the board.

WHAT TO DO

Gather the children together on the carpet and teach them the song 'Thank You For My Friends' from *The Tinderbox* (A&C Black), or teach them the poem on photocopiable page 24. Talk about the different things in the song or poem and the things the children like to do with their friends. Ask questions such as:

- *What type of games do you like to play at playtimes?*
- *What kinds of places do you like to go to together?*
- *What sort of things do you like doing with your friends?*

Explain to the children that together they are going to make a friendship mural; this will be made from the children's own pictures of things they like doing with their friends. Give the children some reflection time in which to consider the pictures they may want to draw, for example a visit to a park, playing football, enjoying a picnic together. Talk quietly about some of the things they may wish to consider. Next, say a short prayer for the children to listen to (the thank-you prayer from the activity 'Friendship cake' on page 18 would be appropriate) and, if you are doing the activity as a whole school, sing 'Thank You Lord for this Fine Day' from *Come and Praise* (BBC publications) particularly the verse 'Thank you Lord for all my friends'.

Organize the children in the place where they will be drawing their pictures (the best place would probably be their own classroom). As they complete their pictures – this could be the next day – ask them to sit in a circle and display their pictures in the centre so that all the children can see them. Again, if you are carrying out the activity as a whole-school assembly, ask one or two children from each class to talk briefly about their pictures. Are there some which have similar themes, for example playing together at playtimes, or taking turns? If there are, group these together and staple a few to the display board. Add an appropriate label to this collection. When you have considered most of the pictures carefully, explain to the children that you will finish the display later for them to share.

Bring the assembly to a close by repeating the song or poem used to introduce it, and sing the same hymn.

SUGGESTIONS FOR DIFFERENTIATION

Talk to the older and more able children about how they feel when their friends are not kind or will not play with them. Are they happy or sad? Do they feel lonely? What could they do when this happens? How do they think their friend feels if they do the same to them? Record some of their ideas to include in the mural.

NOW OR LATER

- Gather the children around the mural and ask them for their ideas to include on the labels. Encourage them to use values such as sharing or taking turns, as well as the names of the games they are playing in the pictures.
- Tell the story of the friendship of Guru Nanak and Mardana in 'The Story of Nanak's Song' in *Gift of a Child* by Michael Grimmitt (Simon and Schuster).

OBJECTIVE
To consider all the things we do together with our friends.

CROSS-CURRICULAR LINKS

ART AND DESIGN
Children could use a range of media to produce the pictures for this assembly including pastels, paint and felt-tipped pens. Relate the lesson to the development of line in an art lesson. When the pictures are finished, ask the children to darken the important lines to give the pictures a clearer outline.

PSHE
This assembly can also contribute well to the children's personal development as they are asked to consider how they felt when their friends were unkind to them.

■ Read the story about David and Jonathan from the Bible (from I Samuel chapters 18–20 and 23 verse 15) to reinforce the children's understanding of friendship.
■ Children could find out about the Buddhist Sangha Day which is linked to friendship and thinking of others.

A CIRCLE OF HANDS

RESOURCES AND ORGANIZATION
You will need: a thank-you prayer, either written by your class together or the one used in the activity 'Friendship cake' on page 18; a display space – this could be a mobile display board covered in your chosen backing paper; a pointer; pieces of paper; skin-tone crayons (available from educational suppliers); scissors; glue. Enlarge the thank-you prayer to a reasonable size and staple it to the centre of the board.

This assembly is best done as a class assembly but could be done as a whole-school assembly with additional adult support.

WHAT TO DO
Gather the children around the board so that they can see the prayer clearly. Read the prayer together following the words with a pointer.

Talk to the children about all the things that we have to be thankful for and explain that together you are going to show this by making a circle of hands. This will show that we are all thankful for our friends, wherever they may be, and that we must all work to make and keep our friends.

Take a piece of paper and draw around your own hand. Show the children how they must colour their hand before cutting it out. Talk about the choice of crayon to get the nearest shade to their skin tone, none of which is white. You may wish to produce a finished hand at this point saying: *I made this one earlier.* Invite the children

to make their own hand templates. (If you are doing this as a school assembly, either arrange for the children to have made their hand templates beforehand or, with additional adult support, organize the children into small groups to carry out this part of the activity.)

When they have finished, invite one or two children, from each class if you are doing it as a whole-school assembly, to attach their hand templates to the board around the prayer so that the fingers are overlapping slightly. Continue until the circle is complete. Collect any unused hands and attach them around the other hands, explaining that these will make the circle stronger. Next, ask the children to join hands and, while they are quiet, talk about the importance of friendship.

Talk about the need to work together to make a friendship strong, how important it is to forgive, love, care, take turns and share. All these things are shown in the circle of hands you have just made together. Use the reflection time as a lead into saying the thank-you prayer together, and sing an appropriate hymn, for example 'He Gave Me Eyes' from *Someone's Singing, Lord* (A&C Black).

SUGGESTIONS FOR DIFFERENTIATION
For very young children, it may be appropriate to do the activity in the classroom with additional adult help, to support the cutting out part of this activity. Brief the adult on how to support the children without doing the task for them. Reinforce the values of friendship during the activity.

NOW OR LATER

■ The children could create a book of prayers on the theme of friendship.
■ Repeat the prayer about being thankful for our friends during other assemblies to reinforce the learning objective.
■ Think about children who might find it difficult to make friends, for example children who speak a different language to the majority, or a newcomer to the group.

GIVING AND RECEIVING

RESOURCES AND ORGANIZATION

You will need: two wrapped presents, one wrapped in plain paper and one wrapped elaborately with bows and a gift tag containing a special message; the storybook *Five Minutes' Peace* by Jill Murphy (Walker Books); an enlarged copy of photocopiable page 25 or individual copies if you want the children to complete them, photocopiable page 26 (for 'Now or later' activity).

This is effective as a whole-school assembly.

WHAT TO DO

Gather the children into a semicircle and talk to them about the occasions when we give and receive presents. As well as birthdays, include multi-faith festivals as well as the traditional Christian celebrations of Easter and Christmas. Show the children the two presents you have wrapped. Explain that you have wrapped them for your friends' birthdays, but you ran out of paper and ribbons when you came to do the second one. Ask the children which present they would like and why. Some children will immediately choose the one that is elaborately wrapped; others will opt for the plainly wrapped one, as they will know you want them to be considerate and thoughtful.

Next, ask the children which one shows your friends that you like them a lot and that you value their friendship. This time the children should come to the conclusion that the elaborately wrapped present would show you really cared about their friendship. Spend a few minutes talking about why this could be the case. Perhaps it is because you have taken the time and trouble to wrap it nicely, or because you have chosen a pretty paper, or one that you know your friend will like.

Now talk to the children about all the things you could give to friends which do not necessarily need money or wrapping in fancy paper. Ask questions such as:
■ *Could we give love? How could we do this?*
■ *Could we offer to play with them or go with them to the dentist, for example?*
■ *Could we offer to share our toys or our games?*
■ *Who thinks they could make their friend a card or a special tea?*

At this point sing an appropriate hymn such as 'Love is Something if You Give it Away' from *Someone's Singing, Lord* (A&C Black).

OBJECTIVE
To learn that when we give a present to our friends, we can show them how special we think they are.

CROSS-CURRICULAR LINKS
DESIGN AND TECHNOLOGY
Children could design wrapping paper as part of a project.

MATHS
Children could make boxes from nets.

Settle the children and tell them that you are going to read a story about a family of elephants who almost found a very good present to give their mum. Read the story *Five Minutes' Peace* by Jill Murphy. At the end of the story, spend a short time reflecting on how the elephants could have given their mum a very good present, and recap some of the things you have discussed during the assembly. As the children think about these things, talk to them quietly about love, kindness, thoughtfulness and valuing friendships by showing friends how much we care for them. Say the following prayer to finish the assembly:

Dear Lord
Help us to show our friends how much we care about our friendship,
When we play together or when we choose a special present for their birthday.
Help us to consider their feelings as well as our own.
Amen.

SUGGESTIONS FOR DIFFERENTIATION

Talk to older and more able children in small groups about some of the presents they have given and received. Which ones did they like/not like? Ask them to give reasons for their opinions.

NOW OR LATER

■ Create an area in the classroom where the children can wrap presents. Leave a selection of tapes and ribbons, scissors, labels and writing implements for the children to use.

■ Photocopiable page 25 requires the children to write down how the pictures show the children are sharing and co-operating with each other. You can either use the sheet with the whole class or give it to children to complete individually.

■ Tell the children about the giving and receiving of gifts during celebrations of festivals of other faiths, for example Eid, Divali and Raksha Bandhan.

■ Read the poem 'A smile' on photocopiable page 26 and use it as a basis for follow-up work in the classroom or for another assembly. It provides a good example of giving a present without cost.

■ Tell the children the story of the little boy who gave the Buddha grains of sand and the Mexican story of the poinsettia in *The Infant Assembly Book* by Doreen Vause (Stanley Thornes).

WHO CAN WE TRUST?

OBJECTIVE
To learn that not everyone is our friend and that we should say 'No' and go when we are approached by strangers.

CROSS-CURRICULAR LINKS
PSHE
This assembly contributes to the children's personal development by raising their awareness of people who are not always their friends and learning to say 'No' and go when meeting someone they do not know.

RESOURCES AND ORGANIZATION

You will need pictures of a number of different people for the main assembly and for the differentiated activity. Try to avoid stereotypes. For example, include a picture of a female police inspector, a male teacher from an ethnic minority group and so on. Alternatively, you could use or include the pictures on photocopiable page 27. Enlarge the pictures before use and display them on a board or use an overhead projector if one is available.

This is an assembly that can be done with the whole school but it is suggested that the ideas presented are reinforced in a class setting when the children will have more opportunity to contribute to the discussions.

WHAT TO DO

Settle the children into an area that lends itself to discussion and where all the children will feel fully involved. This will support the need to listen to, and consider carefully, the difficult issues presented.

Begin the assembly by talking with the children about their friends. Ask them if *all* people are their friends. Explain to the children that although most people are kind and can be trusted, not everyone wants to be their friend.

Show the children one of the pictures, for example the female police inspector and ask them what they can tell you about the person in the picture. What is the person wearing? Can the children tell what job the person does from the clothes being worn? Does the person look friendly? Is this a person the children can trust? Why? Is there a time when we would not know whether or not this person could be trusted? Show the children the picture of the police inspector out of uniform at this point and ask the children if they can be sure that this person can be trusted.

Now show the children the picture of 'mum' and ask them the same questions. This time, though, stress that although a person may be a mum, if they do not know her she is still a stranger and they must never go anywhere with her.

Show the children the picture of the lollipop man and ask them the same sort of questions. Respond to their answers and incorporate their responses into your questions, developing on from their thinking and reinforcing your teaching points.

Stress that although most strangers are probably very kind, they should never go anywhere with them if they do not know them. In fact, they should *never* go anywhere unless their mum or dad knows and has told them personally that it is OK to do so. Reinforce to the children that a stranger is a person we do not know. Do not try to define the issues too finely or this will lead to confusion. It is important for the children to know that if they do not know the person, they can never be trusted. If the person is someone in authority or is someone their parents know, they can sometimes be trusted, and if the person is their teacher or their parent they can usually be trusted.

Finish the assembly with a short moment of reflection, considering how the children should behave when meeting or being approached by someone they do not know. Sing the hymn 'I'm Very Glad of God' from *Someone's Singing, Lord* (A&C Black), and finish with the following prayer:

Dear God
Help me to remember to keep myself safe, to think about things before I do them;
When I am out playing with my friends, shopping in the supermarket or riding my bike in the garden,
Help me to remember to say 'No' and go if I am approached by someone I do not know.
Amen.

SUGGESTIONS FOR DIFFERENTIATION

Discuss the children's thoughts with them and reinforce the learning objective. Talk to the children about who to approach if they get lost or separated from their carer or parent when out on a trip. Many shops and entertainment centres have places where children can go if they get lost. Talk to the children about these.

NOW OR LATER

■ Make a list of all the people that the children can trust.
■ Make posters about the 'say "No" and go' plan when we meet strangers and display these prominently around the school.
■ Read the children some of the traditional tales including 'Little Red Riding Hood' and 'The Wolf and the Seven Little Kids' and talk about the issues of stranger danger contained in these stories.

Friendship poem

For all the times we play our games
Thank you for my friends.
They always share their toys with me,
They often invite me home for tea,
There's nowhere else I'd rather be
Than playing with my friends.

For all the times that they are kind
Thank you for my friends.
They always help when I fall down,
They make me smile when I am down,
When I am mad they calm me down
And help me to make friends.

Giving and receiving

How are these children giving?

How are these children giving?

How are these children giving?

A smile

How much does a smile cost? A penny or a pound?
How sad would your face look without one around?

A smile lights up your face and it lights up your eyes.
It lights up your heart and it lights up your lives.

Could you give a smile for free? And if you did,
What would it do for people like me?

Would your smile light up my face and light up my
                                                    eyes?

Would it light up my heart and light up my life?

How would your smile make me feel?

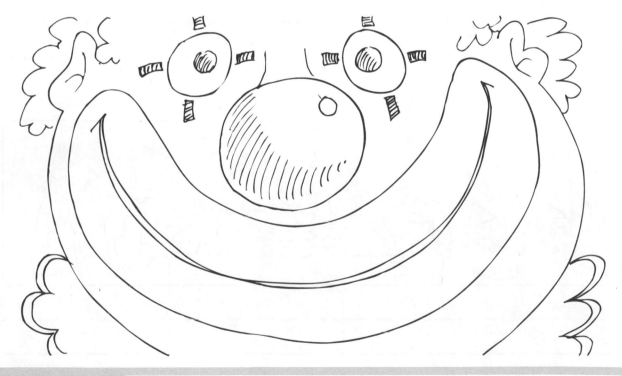

Who can you trust?

Say NO to strangers and GO.

The assemblies in this section focus on children learning to:
- know what to do when someone feels sad
- consider that their actions and conduct have an impact on others
- consider the importance of thinking of others and respecting each other's feelings
- reflect upon their own feelings and say in simple terms how to deal with negative feelings
- develop a consideration for others.

STARTING SCHOOL

OBJECTIVE

To reflect upon their own feelings and how children who have recently started school may be feeling today.

CROSS-CURRICULAR LINKS

GEOGRAPHY

- Make a map of the school buildings and grounds. Pair an older child with one who has just started school and, under adult supervision, ask them to escort the children around the school, showing them where the playground, dining hall and library are for example.
- Link the puppet in this assembly to the QCA geography unit called 'Where in the world is Barnaby Bear?'

RESOURCES AND ORGANIZATION

You will need: a puppet such as a sock puppet or glove puppet (an oven mitt could also be used), a container such as a box or basket in which to keep it, a story or poem about starting school (you could use the one on photocopiable page 35).

This would make an appropriate assembly for the beginning of a new term to the whole school but not when the youngest children are attending for the first time. This assembly links well with the one entitled 'Making rules' on page 56 in this book and they could therefore be carried out as consecutive assemblies.

WHAT TO DO

Welcome the children into assembly and sing the hymn 'At Half Past 3 We Go Home for Tea' from *Someone's Singing, Lord* (A&C Black).

Tell the children that you want to introduce all the people who have started your school this term. There may be teachers and other adults, and older children who have joined from other schools, who are willing to say a few things about themselves and how they are feeling now they have been at the school for a little while. Alternatively, read the poem on photocopiable page 35.

When this has been done, introduce the puppet to the children, explaining that this is his or her first day at school. Pretend to listen to the puppet and repeat what it says! *'You didn't realize there would be so many children at this school?' 'Listen'* again. *'Aren't they big?'* Reassure the puppet and ask how it is feeling. Is it excited? Listen to the puppet while it gives you its response, repeating what is said. *You're excited because you are looking forward to learning new things/making new friends/playing in the playground.* Ask the puppet if it is looking forward to PE and staying for dinner. Depending on your situation, you may want the puppet to raise a few doubts. For

example, it may be looking forward to PE but is worried that it will not be able to find its PE kit in the cloakroom, or not be able to do up its buttons and shoelaces when getting dressed. Handle these issues sensitively and positively by inviting the older children to suggest ways of dealing with these things.

Ask the children if they would like to ask the puppet anything about how it is feeling. Repeat each question to the puppet and, pretending to listen to the reply, respond appropriately to the children's questions. You may have to be creative here!

Finally, ask the puppet if it is worried about anything. You may wish to address the following issues:

■ What to do when you want the toilet.
■ Not being able to find your way somewhere.
■ Coping with 'big' children in the playground.
■ Finding your belongings at hometime.

You may wish to ask the children who have recently started school how they feel at this point. Encourage positive feelings, as you do not want the children leaving assembly feeling unhappy. Spend some time reflecting on how the new children must be feeling today and how you can support one another. Talk about what to do if a new child is alone in the playground – encourage the child to smile and talk about themselves, or perhaps take them to an adult for reassurance. Finish this period of reflection with your school prayer if you have one, or use the traditional 'This is our school' prayer, opposite.

This is our school.
Let peace dwell here,
Let the room be full
of happiness,
Let love abide here,
Love of one another,
Love of mankind,
Love of life itself,
And love of God.
Let us remember
That, as many hands
build a house,
So many hearts make
a school.

Sing a lively and happy hymn such as 'Stand Up, Clap Hands' from *Someone's Singing, Lord* (A&C Black) or 'This Little Light of Mine' from *Junior Praise* (Marshall Pickering) and finish the assembly by welcoming all the new people to your school.

SUGGESTIONS FOR DIFFERENTIATION

Some of the more confident new children may be happy to contribute to the assembly by saying a little about themselves and how much they have been looking forward to starting school. Use these children as a starting point for the assembly. Follow up the discussions with the new children in their classroom during the day, taking care not to unsettle any less confident children.

NOW OR LATER

■ Allow any children who wish to, to talk about their feelings when they started school. These may include some children who have just started. Encourage them to talk about all the things they like about school.
■ With the children, write a school prayer incorporating all the values you wish to promote.
■ Talk about the mixed feelings of children who may be new to the area or country.

WE ARE ALL DIFFERENT, BUT WE ALL HAVE FEELINGS

RESOURCES AND ORGANIZATION

You will need: a collection of felt-tipped pens which look different on the outside but all contain grey ink; a copy of *Elmer – The Story of a Patchwork Elephant* by David McKee (Red Fox); flip chart; a copy of photocopiable page 36 for each child (for 'Now or later' activity).

This can be conducted as a whole school assembly with the issues being discussed in smaller class groups as a follow-up activity or, alternatively, it can be held over two days to the whole school.

WHAT TO DO

Settle the children so that they can see the flip chart and the pens and begin the assembly by asking them to tell you something about themselves that is different to someone else. Do they have different hair or eye colour? Are they taller than their friend, have longer hair and so on? Tell the children that today you are going to consider how, although people may look different, they all have feelings, and they probably feel the same way about certain things. At this point, read *Elmer*.

OBJECTIVE

To reflect upon the feelings of others and to begin to realize that although we all look different, we all have the same feelings.

CROSS-CURRICULAR LINKS

ART AND DESIGN

Use elephant templates to develop the children's handwriting skills by asking them to create their own patterned elephants for 'Elmer's Day'.

When you have finished the story, discuss with the children how Elmer felt. *Did he like being different at the beginning of the story? What did he do? Did he change his mind?* Discuss the reasons why he changed his mind, reinforcing the learning objective that although he looked different to the other elephants he still had the same feelings. He felt sad because he thought he wasn't the same as the other elephants and needed support to feel wanted. *How did the other elephants make him feel better about himself?*

Talk to the children about how they feel at this point. Do they feel different at all? When and what makes them feel different? How do they feel about this? This may develop into a deeper discussion at this point. If it does, give the children the opportunity to talk about different sorts of issues; these may include incidents of racial behaviour and bullying. Make it clear that these are unacceptable, and discuss with the children what they should do if they see or experience such behaviour. Allow discussions to develop and finish with the hymn and prayer suggested below. After the assembly, follow up with the 'spot the difference, we are the same' activity on photocopiable page 36.

Should you decide not to develop the discussion, continue the assembly.

Draw a picture of an elephant on the flip chart and tell the children that you are going to use the pens to colour in the picture of Elmer. Show the children the pens and ask them to describe them to you. Elicit from them the fact that the pens are all different colours and that they all look different.

Invite a child to choose a pen and colour in one of Elmer's ears. As this is being done, ask another child to choose a different pen and to colour one of his legs. Continue in this way until there is no more space for the children to colour Elmer comfortably. The children should start to notice that although the pens appear to be different colours on the outside, the ink is the same and that they are colouring in an ordinary grey elephant. If not, point this out. Reinforce the learning objective and explain that although people may look different we must treat each other the same because we all have the same feelings.

The hymns 'When I Needed a Neighbour' or 'The Ink is Black, the Page is White', from *Someone's Singing, Lord* (A&C Black), will give you the basis for a short period of reflection. Encourage the children to think quietly about the issues of how we treat people who look different to ourselves. Bring the assembly to a close with the following prayer:

Dear Lord
Help me to treat other people in the way that I would like to be treated. Help me to remember that just as I have feelings, so they have feelings too. Amen.

SUGGESTIONS FOR DIFFERENTIATION

Before the assembly, ask the children to draw pictures of themselves using 'people' crayons (available from educational suppliers) and display these as a portrait gallery. Use the pictures to discuss the things that are different about us and staple the children's suggestions on labels above the pictures. Underneath, display labels with words describing the feelings the children have experienced such as 'happy', 'sad', 'thankful', 'relieved'. Add the title 'Although we look different, we have the same feelings'.

NOW OR LATER

■ Ask children to complete the activity on photocopiable page 36. They can draw circles around the differences or tell a partner and and then write down a couple of ways in which the children in the picture are the same (obviously not just referring to physical similarities).

■ Talk about the lives of people such as Martin Luther King and Gandhi who worked tirelessly for equality.

■ Read the story of the Good Samaritan from the Bible (Luke 10, verses 30–37).

■ Relate the theme of the assembly to the story of 'Beauty and the Beast'.

■ Tell the traditional Indian story of Bhola (or Rupa) the elephant who was tired of being grey and wanted to have bright colours. The story will be available in libraries with specialist Indian collections but goes something like this:

Bhola lived in a zoo and gave rides to the children who loved him. However, he grew tired of being grey, so his friend – a bird – went to the other animals and borrowed stripes from the tiger, bright colours from the parrot, feathers from the peacock, spots from the leopard, and so on. Bhola was delighted, but when the children came to the zoo they didn't recognize him. They were scared of this new elephant and wanted Bhola back. So Bhola went back to being grey.

LOST AND FOUND

RESOURCES AND ORGANIZATION
You will need: a copy of photocopiable page 37 for each child, plus an enlarged copy or an OHT, a display board or overhead projector; a felt-tipped or OHP pen.

WHAT TO DO
Settle the children and explain that you are going to tell them a story about a brother and sister who went shopping with their mum. Begin the story at this point.

Susan and Scott had been looking forward to going shopping with their mum to the new supermarket which was opening down the road. Every day on their way to school they had walked past it and watched it being built. Today was the day of the grand opening.
   As they arrived, they noticed that the car park was nearly full.
   'There must be lots of people doing their shopping today,' Mum remarked.
   Eventually they found a parking space and made their way to the main entrance. People were already leaving with trolleys full of goodies.
   'Look!' exclaimed Susan excitedly, 'they're giving away balloons.' Sure enough, their friend Max came out of the store clutching a big blue balloon. He told them that someone in the store was giving away blue and red balloons.
   'Yippee!' said Scott. 'Maybe we'll get one. I want a blue one. Which colour do you want Susan?'
   'I think I'd like a red one,' she replied.
   When they got inside the store, Mum reminded them both to stay close to her side as the shop was so busy. She didn't want the children to get lost in the new store.

   Stop the story at this point and ask the children if they think Scott and Susan were listening to their mum. They will probably make many suggestions, but try to conclude that they possibly were not listening, or may forget what mum had said, because they were so excited about getting a balloon, which was all they could think about. Continue with the story.

OBJECTIVE
To think about the feelings of others and begin to learn how to deal with their own feelings.

CROSS-CURRICULAR LINKS
PSHE
This assembly would link well with the theme of keeping safe.

They started to do the shopping and at first Scott and Susan helped Mum put lots of things into the trolley. They chose fruit, their favourite yoghurts and lots of treats. When they got to the delicatessen counter, Mum was very busy asking the assistant for the things that she wanted. Susan and Scott started to get bored and looked around. Scott noticed a huge cloud of red and blue balloons sailing above the shelves in the distance. He turned to his sister, 'Come on, Susan,' he said. 'They're only over there and Mum will be ages yet. We'll get there and back before she's finished.'

Scott and Susan walked to the aisle where Scott had seen the balloons, but they were nowhere to be seen. They looked back at the delicatessen counter and yes, Mum was still there. Scott looked and there were the balloons hovering above the shelves in the next aisle.

'It'll be fine,' said Scott. 'We'll be there and back before Mum has finished,' so off they went down the aisle in search of the balloons.

The children may react at this point of the story and there may be an opportunity to talk about what the children should have done.

When Scott and Susan reached the place where they thought they'd seen the balloons, there were none to be seen. Where had they gone?

'There they are,' shouted Scott and he set off in the direction of the balloons. Susan had to run to keep up. Every time they got to the place where they had seen the balloons, they had moved to another part of the store!

'Perhaps we should go back,' suggested Susan. She looked around and found to her dismay that she didn't know which way to go. They were lost.

Ask the children how they think Scott and Susan felt when they discovered they were lost. What do the children think Scott and Susan did next? You may or may not wish to record the children's suggestions. Continue with the story.

In the meantime, Mum had finished at the delicatessen counter and turned to leave. Where were Scott and Susan? She had told them to stay with her.

Ask the children how they think Mum felt at this point. They should make suggestions such as cross, sad, upset, worried. What do they think Mum did next? Continue with the story.

Scott and Susan began to cry. One of the people who worked at the supermarket asked them what was the matter but they were crying so much that they couldn't tell her, all they could do was say their name. She took them to the customer service desk and made an announcement.

'Would Mrs Cooke come to the customer service desk immediately please?'

Mum guessed what had happened and hurried to the service desk where she saw Scott and Susan crying but safe.

Talk to the children about how Scott, Susan and Mum probably felt at this time. How do they think Scott and Susan felt when they saw Mum? How did Mum feel when she saw Scott and Susan were safe? What do they think she said and did? Finish the story.

When Scott and Susan saw Mum, they ran to her and wrapped their arms around her.

'What a relief,' said Mum. 'You had me really worried. I'm very glad I've found you.'

Just at that moment the person carrying the balloons walked past and asked Scott and Susan if they would like a balloon.

'Can I have a blue one please?' asked Scott.

'Can I have a red one please?' said Susan.

At the end of the story, ask the children if they have ever been lost. How did they feel? How did they feel when they were found? How did their mum feel? Display the enlarged copy of photocopiable page 37 on a display board or an overhead projector and complete the speech bubbles with the children. Talk about what Scott and Susan should have done instead of going to look for the balloons. What should the children do if they ever become separated from their parent when they are out?

The hymn 'Thank You Lord for this Fine Day' from *Someone's Singing, Lord* (A&C Black) is appropriate to support the theme of this assembly. Make up a verse 'Thank you Lord for keeping me safe'.

Finish the assembly by saying the following prayer:

Dear Lord
Help us to be sensible when we go out with our families and friends. Help me to listen to my mum and dad and to stay together all the time. Help me to remember how to keep myself safe.
Amen.

SUGGESTIONS FOR DIFFERENTIATION

Invite three children to act out the story as you read it, showing how the children and Mum felt when the children were lost and then found.

NOW OR LATER

■ Talk to the children about some of the other places or times when it is easy to get separated from their parent or guardian and discuss what they should do if this ever happens to them.

■ Give each child a copy of photocopiable page 37 to complete individually.

THANK YOU FOR MAKING ME ME

OBJECTIVE
To learn to be thankful for who we are and the things we can do.

CROSS-CURRICULAR LINKS
ENGLISH
Use the story during the Literacy Hour when you are looking at traditional tales.

RESOURCES AND ORGANIZATION
You will need: the story of the Ugly Duckling. There are many versions of this traditional tale.

This is equally effective conducted with the whole school or to class groups.

WHAT TO DO

When the children are settled, read them the story of the Ugly Duckling. Stop at appropriate points in the story to discuss how the Ugly Duckling was feeling. How do the children think he felt when the animals made fun of him because of the way he looked? How do the children think the other animals should have behaved? What would they have done if they had seen the Ugly Duckling looking so unhappy?

Finish the assembly by reflecting on all the things that we have to be thankful for. Reinforce the learning objective by recalling some of the talents that the children have, the kindness they have shown and how proud and pleased you are that this is a happy school where everyone gets on so well together.

Finally sing the hymn 'If I Were a Butterfly' from *Junior Praise* (Marshall Pickering) and say the following prayer:

Thank you Lord for making me me.
Thank you for my friends who play with me,
For my toys, clothes and other possessions.
Thank you for the food we have to eat and water to drink
Today and everyday.
Help us to remember other children in this country and around the world who may not have enough food to eat, water to drink, toys to play with and clothes to wear.
Teach me to be grateful for all the things I have.
Thank you for making me me.
Amen.

SUGGESTIONS FOR DIFFERENTIATION
Tell the children a personal tale that makes you glad that you are you – perhaps how grateful you are for your family and friends, or that you are a teacher at that school. Ask the children if they have ever wished that they were someone else and to tell you why. Discuss the implications of this with them and help them to understand that it is much better to be who they are for lots of reasons; for instance they may not have met you if they had been someone else!

NOW OR LATER
■ Talk about other traditional tales in which the main character becomes someone else at the end such as 'Beauty and the Beast', 'The Frog Prince'.
■ Make a story frieze showing the Ugly Duckling's transformation.
■ Relate the story to the stories of Elmer and Bhola (or Rupa).

Starting school

Today is my very first day in school.
How am I feeling? Do I feel cool?
Lost and bewildered, excited and glad.
I've said goodbye to Mum and now I feel sad.

Where is my classroom? Where is my seat?
Where are the toilets? Where will I eat?
How do I find my way out to play?
Mum said my teacher will help me today.

My classroom is bright and full of good things.
We can play lots of games and do other things.
I can go to the playground and play with my friends.
I think I may come here tomorrow again.

Ready to go! **IDEAS FOR ASSEMBLIES**

We are all different

■ Spot the differences:

■ Tell a friend how the children are different.
■ Write how they could be the same.

They both _____

_____

_____

_____

They both _____

_____

_____

Photocopiables

Lost and found

■ Inside the speech bubbles, write down what you think Scott, Susan and Mum might be saying now that they have found each other.

Section 4

The assemblies in this section focus on children learning to:
- develop an awareness of self and raise self-esteem
- develop awareness that they are special to their family and friends
- give reasons for their actions
- reflect upon their actions and the impact upon others
- develop a consideration of others.

I AM SPECIAL

OBJECTIVE
To learn that we all have something special to offer.

CROSS-CURRICULAR LINKS
DESIGN AND TECHNOLOGY
Make sock puppets.

ENGLISH/PSHE
Use the puppets to support speaking and listening and personal and social development by allowing the children to invent role-play situations which they can perform to their class or friends.

RESOURCES AND ORGANIZATION

Make a note of one or two special deeds that you have noticed children doing during the previous week. For example, 'I saw Katie hang someone else's coat on the peg yesterday', 'I saw Connor comfort Amy when she was upset', 'Leon always gives me his special smile', and so on. You will need a sock or a glove puppet, which can be manipulated with your hand inside its mouth and a large container such as a box or basket in which to keep it. Make a copy of photocopiable page 44, one for each child (for 'Now or later' activity).

This is an effective assembly to conduct with the whole school.

WHAT TO DO

Gather the children together in a semicircle and sing the hymn 'If I Were a Butterfly' from *Junior Praise* (Marshall Pickering).

Sit on a chair with the box containing the puppet at your side and where it can be easily accessed. Reach into the box, place your hand inside the puppet's mouth and remove it from the box. Place the puppet's mouth to your ear and pretend that the puppet is speaking to you. Repeat what it says. Pretend that the puppet is upset because it feels it is not special and cannot do anything special. Continue with the following conversation:

What do you mean you cannot do anything special? Everyone can do at least one thing that's special.
Pretend to listen to the puppet's response, repeating what it says as follows:
You say you cannot play football?
Listen to the puppet. *Every time you go to kick the ball you fall over?*
Address the children at this point and say something like:
Well we can't all be good at football, can we?
Listen to the puppet again and continue the conversation something like this:
You can't say your two times table? Listen to the puppet.
When you count in twos, you say 2, 4, 6, 8, 9?'
Manipulate the puppet so that it looks sad.
Don't be sad. Everyone has something special to offer. Why only last week I saw… and repeat one of the kindnesses that you observed during the previous week. *That was a very special thing to do.*
Let's have a good think about some things you have and can do which are special. Look; John is smiling. He is pleased that you came to assembly this morning.

At this point, ask the children how they think the puppet is special. What kind of special qualities does it have? Ask the puppet if it feels special now and manipulate it so that it nods.

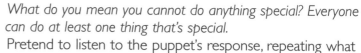

Invite the children to talk about their special qualities and the special things they can do. Is it a sense of humour, a smile, being helpful and kind? Spend a few moments reflecting on all the special qualities the children have thought of before saying the prayer, opposite.

Finish the assembly by singing 'This Little Light of Mine' from *Junior Praise* (Marshall Pickering).

Dear God
Help us to remember that we are all special in at least one way.
Help us to recognize the special qualities in others
And be thankful that we are all different and all special.
Amen.

SUGGESTIONS FOR DIFFERENTIATION

Introduce the assembly by talking about some of the things that make you special. Perhaps you have a special talent or always remember to say thank you, for example. This will set the assembly within a real context.

NOW OR LATER

■ Allow the children to play with puppets over the next few days. Many will tell the puppet all the things they are good at and why they are special, which you or another adult can record.

■ Make a list of all the special qualities the children in each class have.

■ This assembly fits well with the Christmas story and the birth of Jesus, or the births of Krishna, Rama and the Buddha. Discuss why Jesus is special to Christian believers.

■ Talk about the special things that Jesus taught us.

■ Read the children stories from different faiths about special people such as Rama, Guru Nanak, Muhammad or the Buddha.

■ Talk about the special occasions in life such as weddings, birthdays and naming ceremonies.

■ Give each child a copy of photocopiable page 44. This requires them to draw a picture or write about a special deed they have done and to write or draw how they are special.

I CAN DO

RESOURCES AND ORGANIZATION

You will need: a display space; pieces of paper measuring approximately 10cm squared; colouring materials; a staple gun or sticky tape; a copy of photocopiable page 45, one for each child (for 'Now or later' activity). Arrange for one or two adults to perform some of their special talents during the assembly.

This assembly is equally good as a whole-school, key-stage or class assembly.

WHAT TO DO

When the children have settled and been welcomed into assembly, begin by singing the hymn 'This Little Light of Mine' from *Junior Praise* (Marshall Pickering). Explain that you chose that hymn this morning because you want to think about all the things that the children can do. Stress that you do not just mean things like being able to walk and talk, as most of us are able to do these things. You want them to consider all the things that they have worked very hard to learn.

OBJECTIVE
To learn that we can all do lots of important and worthwhile things.

CROSS-CURRICULAR LINKS
PE/Music
Use your knowledge of the children to develop 'I can' activities. Allow them to perform their special talents for the other children to evaluate and copy. Ensure that you choose activities which will allow all children to 'shine'.

Tell the children about some special talent that you have. For example, you may be able to play a musical instrument, be a tennis enthusiast, write poetry, or have a good sense of direction. Perform some of your special talents if you are able, or play a video of some of your accomplishments. You may be able to persuade a colleague to participate also, either to show their special talent or to complement yours.

Read one of the stories from the Bible which depicts one of the special things that Jesus did. For example, the story of Blind Bartemeus (Mark 10, verses 46–52), healing the leper (Luke 5, verses 12–16), or feeding the five thousand (Luke 9, verses 10–17). Talk about the fact that Jesus is a special person to Christians because He was a very special teacher and because of the things He could do.

Ask the children to think about their own special talents. What can they do that they are particularly proud of? As the children reflect, remind them that these can be things that they do out of school, perhaps swimming, football or sponsored walks. After a short time, ask the children for their contributions and invite one or two from each class to share their thoughts with everyone. You may find it appropriate at this point to talk about the Sikh festival of Hola Maholla in which people show off their individual talents in poetry, music or sporting competitions.

Show the children the squares of paper and explain that after assembly you want them to draw a picture of one thing that they can do. Explain that you will collect their pictures and use them to make an 'I can' display on the board. When it is completed, leave the display board in a prominent place so that the children can look at each other's work.

Finish the assembly with the prayer below.

SUGGESTIONS FOR DIFFERENTIATION

Be aware of and sensitive to children who may have specific difficulties and include these children in the assembly. Their contribution may be greater than others' because they have to overcome additional difficulties.

Find out before the assembly about any children who have achieved awards outside school, for example piano grades, swimming badges, charity walks, and so on. Include these in the assembly.

> Dear God
> Thank you for the special talents that I have.
> Help me to share them with others.
> Show me how to appreciate the talents of others
> So that I may learn from them too.
> Amen.

NOW OR LATER

■ Conduct an assembly about hobbies and encourage the children to talk about the things that they do.

■ Make a list of all the things the children do over a week or two. Cover all the things they do at home as well as at school.

■ Make an 'I can' wall onto which the children can display their pictures and writing about the things they can do. Give each child a copy of photocopiable page 45. This requires them to draw or write about some of the things they can do and will support this assembly.

THE LOST SHEEP

RESOURCES AND ORGANIZATION

You will need the story of the shepherd and the lost sheep from the New Testament (Luke 15, verses 1–7), adhesive tape, ten copies of photocopiable page 46 to make 100 pictures of sheep. Display 95 sheep in rows on a board and hide five around the hall or area where the assembly is to be conducted. Good places to hide the sheep are on a piece of PE apparatus, in the bottom corner of a window, on the back of the piano, behind an item of furniture and underneath the seat of the chair on which you will be sitting. This assembly is best conducted with the whole school. Allow class groups the opportunity to look for the missing sheep after the assembly.

WHAT TO DO

When the children are settled, draw their attention to the rows of sheep and explain that there should be 100. Count the sheep together, or ask a child to come out and to point to each sheep in turn while you all count them. When you have finished, look puzzled and comment that there are some missing. Ask the children how many are missing. By now, some children may have noticed a few of the hidden sheep. Tell them not to shout out but to indicate if they can see any of them. Ask children, in turn, to fetch one of the sheep and attach it to the board. Continue until all the easily noticeable sheep have been collected. Look perplexed and indicate that there is still one missing. (This is the one which is taped to the underside of your chair. If you think the children will find it there put it in your pocket.)

Explain to the children that there is a story in the Bible, which Jesus told, about a shepherd who had lost a sheep. Read the story to the children at this point. At the end, emphasize that Jesus told the story to explain to people that, just as the shepherd was overjoyed when he had found all of his sheep, so God is happy when we are all one of his flock and have learned not to do things that are wrong.

At this point ask the children, without allowing them to move, to have a good look around. Can they find the missing sheep now? Reflect upon the story and the message it gives. Repeat the verses from Luke, using more familiar language for the children to understand, and remind them how important it is to own up to any wrongdoings. Tell them how happy people are when this happens.

Sing the hymn 'Lost and Found' from *Come and Praise* (BBC publications) and say a short prayer to finish the assembly.

If the sheep has not been found by the end of assembly, move it once the children have left, to a more visible place. This could be, for example, behind some PE apparatus which you know a class will be using, or in among the large balls which will be used at playtime. Wait for the excitement when the sheep is found.

OBJECTIVE
To learn that we are all special in the eyes of God.

CROSS-CURRICULAR LINKS
MATHS
Use the sheep as a basis for counting activities, counting in ones, twos and fives. Organize the 95 sheep in rows of ten and use the display to introduce the idea of grouping in tens to count large numbers of items.

SUGGESTIONS FOR DIFFERENTIATION

Talk to the children in small groups about all the times that they have done something wrong but have been unable to talk about it. How did they feel about it? Reinforce to them that it is always better to own up to wrongdoings because not only will others feel happy, they, also, will feel better.

NOW OR LATER

■ Read other stories from the Bible which reflect the admission of wrongdoing and forgiveness, for example the Prodigal Son (Luke 15, verses 11–32).
■ Find out about Yom Kippur and Ramadan which are periods of reflection.

THINKING FOR MYSELF

OBJECTIVE

To understand the need to think for yourself when making decisions.

CROSS-CURRICULAR LINKS
PSHE

Set up a series of problem-solving activities which will develop the children's abilities to think things through for themselves.

RESOURCES AND ORGANIZATION

You will need: the traditional story called 'Careless Hans' (a version of this story is provided below).

This assembly is best conducted with the whole school.

WHAT TO DO

Gather the children together in a circle and talk about the importance of thinking for yourself, especially if someone is trying to get you to do something which is wrong. Explain that you are going to tell them a story about a boy who, although he did not do anything wrong, got into all kinds of scrapes because he did not think for himself. Begin the story at this point.

One day, Careless Hans went to visit his grandmother who lived on the other side of the village. When it was time to go, she asked him to take a needle and thread home to his mother who had contacted her to say she had run out of white cotton and needed to sew a button on Hans' shirt. On

the way home, Hans noticed that the farmer had finished haymaking and there were a number of hay bales waiting to be collected and taken to the barn. Hans stopped to have a rest and to keep the needle safe, put it into one of the hay bales. When it was time for Hans to go home though, he could not find the needle. 'Silly Hans,' said his mother. 'Why didn't you thread the needle through your collar to keep it safe?' 'I'll remember that,' thought Hans.

The next time Hans visited his grandmother, she gave him a handkerchief as a present for his mother's birthday. Hans remembered what his mother had said and threaded the handkerchief through his collar. When he got home, the handkerchief had fallen off and was nowhere to be seen. 'Silly Hans,' said his mother, 'Why didn't you put it in your pocket to keep it safe?' 'I'll remember that,' thought Hans.

The next time Hans went to his grandmother's house, she gave him a puppy which needed a new home. Guess what he did to keep it safe? He put it in his pocket and when he got home the poor dog was very stiff and upset. 'Silly Hans', said his mother. 'Why didn't you put some string around his neck and lead him along behind you?' 'I'll remember that', thought Hans.

The next time Hans visited his grandmother, she gave him a joint of meat for his tea. He tied a piece of string to the meat and dragged it along behind him. When he got home there was only a scraggy bit of meat left. The rest had been eaten by all

the cats and dogs of the village who had been chewing at it as he walked back. 'Silly Hans,' said his mother. 'Why didn't you put it in a brown paper parcel and tie it to your head?' 'I'll remember that,' thought Hans.

The next time he went to his grandmother's house, she gave Hans some butter to take home. Hans remembered what his mother had said. He wrapped it in brown paper and tied it to his head. Now it was the middle of summer and it was a very hot day. The sun shone down on Hans and the butter began to melt. Soon it was running into his hair, dripping into his ears and eyes and running down his neck. By the time Hans arrived home, all the butter had melted and Hans was in a dreadful mess! 'Silly Hans,' said his mother. 'When are you going to start thinking for yourself?' And after that he did.

At the end of the story, talk to the children about the importance of thinking for themselves. Discuss times when it can be dangerous if they do not think for themselves, for example, when they need to cross the road or are out on their bike. Remind the children about thinking for themselves when caring for the environment, for example, by looking after the plants in the garden and not dropping litter in the street, and tidying away at the end of activities and not suddenly needing to go to the toilet. You may also be able to link the theme to stranger danger.

Finish the assembly by singing 'He Gave Me Eyes' from *Someone's Singing, Lord* (A&C Black) and say a prayer (see right).

Dear Lord
Help me to think for myself by reminding me to do the right thing even when my brain is telling me to do something else.
Help me to remember not to drop litter, to tidy things away and to look after my things and my school.
Thank you for helping me to do all these things.
Amen.

SUGGESTIONS FOR DIFFERENTIATION

Talk to the children about the times when they have been in trouble because they have copied someone else's behaviour rather than thinking for themselves about how to behave. Perhaps they have forgotten how to be kind to others, knocked a coat off a peg and not picked it up, or broken one of the school rules. Reinforce the importance of thinking for themselves.

NOW OR LATER

■ Make a list of all the times the children have remembered to think for themselves. Make a target of, for example, 20 occasions for the children to receive a special treat – perhaps listening to their favourite story.

■ Read the traditional tale 'The Miller, His Son and the Donkey' which centres around a similar theme, or *Lazy Jack* by Tony Ross (Puffin Books).

I am special

What have you done this week?
■ Write or draw inside the boxes.

I have

I helped

I am special because

I can do

■ Write or draw what you can do.

I can write my name. _____

I can count to _____

I can play with my friends.   I am kind to

I can look after my things.

The lost sheep

WORKING TOGETHER

The assemblies in this section focus on children learning to:
■ think of others
■ reflect upon their actions and conduct at school and at home
■ say why they think they should behave in a certain way
■ talk about why we should help others.

HELPING OUT

RESOURCES AND ORGANIZATION

You will need: a copy of the story 'The Little Red Hen' provided on photocopiable page 54; a copy of photocopiable page 55, one for each child (for 'Now or later').

This is an effective assembly to deliver to the whole school, or as a class assembly performed to the school. Give children in the class parts to play and ask the other children to read different parts of the narrative, for example saying the prayer and introducing the hymn. A short follow-up activity is required.

WHAT TO DO

Invite the children to tell you about the kind of things that they like to help with at home and at school. Do they like helping to clean the windows, the car or their bedroom? Maybe they like to help with the cooking, shopping or gardening? Why do they like helping with the things that they do? For example, perhaps they like helping with the cooking because they like to eat the things afterwards.

Read the story of the Little Red Hen on photocopiable page 54 at this point.

At the end of the story, ask the children the following questions:

■ *How do you think the Little Red Hen felt when the three animals refused to help plant the corn?*

■ *Do you think she had already decided that she would not share the cake if they did not help?*

■ *Do you think she would have given them another chance to share the cake if they had offered to help her make it?*

■ *How do you think the three animals felt when the Little Red Hen refused to share the cake?*

■ *How do you think the Little Red Hen felt when she was eating the cake?*

■ *Do you think the three animals will help the Little Red Hen when she wants to plant the seeds next year?*

■ *What would you have done if the Little Red Hen had asked you to help?*

Give the children an opportunity to consider the last time they were asked to help someone and refused. How would they behave now? Would they help the next time they were asked? While the children are still and quiet, say an appropriate prayer or make one up. Finish the assembly by singing 'When I Needed a Neighbour' from *Someone's Singing, Lord* (A&C Black).

OBJECTIVE

To consider the importance of helping if we can and to think of others as well as ourselves.

CROSS-CURRICULAR LINKS

SCIENCE

Plant seeds as a science activity and record their growth.

ENGLISH

Rewrite the story as a playscript or a poem with the children as a class or group activity.

SUGGESTIONS FOR DIFFERENTIATION

Organize a group of children to act out the story. Stop the story at appropriate points to discuss what the three animals should do. Should they help the Little Red Hen? Encourage the more able children to think of an alternative ending to the story. For instance, what do they think would have happened if the three friends had offered to help make the cake? Or if they had decided that although they did not help to make the cake they would help to eat it anyway? What if the Little Red Hen had agreed to share the cake? What impact do the children think this would have had on the animals' attitude? Do they think that the three animals would have helped the next year, or do they think they would not have learned their lesson?

NOW OR LATER

■ Give each child a copy of photocopiable page 55 and ask them to complete the thought bubbles for each of the three animals as they watch the Little Red Hen eat the cake.

■ Read the story from the Bible about the Good Samaritan (Luke 10, verses 30–37).

■ Ask the children to draw or paint pictures of the various ways they like to help. Display the pictures in a prominent place.

■ Talk about the different ways people give thanks for the harvest, including Sukkot and the yam harvest. This is celebrated in West Africa and celebrates the first of the yam crop. It is celebrated by families getting together, masked dancing and food.

WE ALL HAVE A PART TO PLAY

OBJECTIVE

To learn that everyone's contribution is important.

CROSS-CURRICULAR LINKS

DESIGN AND TECHNOLOGY

Organize menus for a party including a recipe for fruit punch.

ENGLISH/MATHS

Write invitations to the party and work out how much it is going to cost for all the food and drink.

RESOURCES AND ORGANIZATION

You will need: several used fruit juice bottles and cartons filled with water; a container such as a basin, large enough to hold the water contained in the bottles and cartons; a table on which to display them; a ladle and a few plastic goblets.

This is an effective whole-school assembly, which requires some follow-up class discussions.

WHAT TO DO

When the children are settled, explain that you are going to tell them a story to show how everyone's contribution is important.

Set the following scene:

It was the day of Grandma's birthday and all the family were going to be there to celebrate. Everyone was getting ready to leave. They were all dressed in their best clothes and they had the party food and drinks ready. Or did they?

The planning for Grandma's 80th birthday had taken place four weeks ago. Aunty Jenny had agreed to make the birthday cake, Uncle Joe was making a trifle, Cousin Jim was going to provide the fruit salad and Aunty Tracey the black forest gateau. Everyone had agreed to make sandwiches and bring along some sausage rolls. They were also going to make a fruit punch. Everyone agreed to bring fruit juice to the party which they would pour into a huge bowl from which people could help themselves.

At this point in the assembly, place the empty punchbowl on the table, then continue with the story.

Aunty Jenny had bought three bottles of fruit juice for the fruit punch. She had bought them a few days before and had put them in the fridge until the day of the party. One night, Michael, Aunty Jenny's son, came home from work and was so

thirsty that he drank a whole bottle of fruit juice in one go. 'Oh no,' thought Michael. Then he had an idea. 'I'll fill the bottle with water,' he thought. 'When everyone has poured their bottles of fruit juice into the punch, no one will know if one of them has been filled with water.'

The next morning, Uncle Fred, Aunty Jenny's husband, got up late to go to work. He looked in the fridge for something to drink, and guess what? He saw the fruit juice. 'It won't matter if I drink one of these bottles of fruit juice. I'll fill the bottle with water and when everyone pours the fruit juice into the punch no one will notice if one of them is filled with water.'

Later that morning, Aunty Jenny's next-door neighbour came to visit. Aunty Jenny offered to make a cup of coffee but when she looked in the cupboard, there was no coffee left. Instead, she offered her friend a drink of fruit juice. By the end of the morning the bottle of fruit juice was empty. 'Never mind' thought Aunty Jenny. I'll just fill the bottle with water. No one will notice if one of them is filled with water because everyone else's will be full of fruit juice.

The same thing happened at Uncle Joe's, Cousin Jim's and Aunty Tracey's. They had all drunk the fruit juice and had filled the bottles with water. They had all thought the same thing: 'It doesn't matter if mine is filled with water because everyone else's will be fruit juice.'

They all arrived at the party.

At this point invite several children to play the part of the people in the story. Supervise them as they pour their 'fruit juice' into the punchbowl.

Invite one of the children to be Grandma. Ask 'Grandma' if she would like a drink of the special fruit punch that her children had made for her very special birthday. Continue with the story.

All of the guests were smiling because they thought everyone else had filled the punchbowl with fruit juice and only their carton was filled with water. Grandma tasted the fruit punch. 'This is water,' she cried.

Spend a short time reflecting on how the children think Grandma felt. Do they think she felt special? Why did all the people think that their contribution was not important? What do the children think the people learned from this lesson?

Say a short prayer and sing 'The Building Song' from *Come and Praise* (BBC publications).

SUGGESTIONS FOR DIFFERENTIATION

For less able children, reinforce the concept by repeating the theme of the assembly using another context, for example making a fruit salad or a vegetable stew which turns out to only contain water. Ask the more able children to think of a story to tell their classmates about how important everyone's contribution is.

NOW OR LATER

■ Make a list of all the times when the children's contribution is important. Times will become evident during the day, but occasions could include getting out the PE apparatus, writing a class poem or story in which everyone makes up a line, or making a get-well card for someone who is ill.

■ Tell the stories of the Enormous Watermelon and the Enormous Turnip which illustrate the importance of the contribution made by small people or animals.

LEARNING TO WORK TOGETHER

OBJECTIVE

To learn how important it is to work together to do some jobs properly.

CROSS-CURRICULAR LINKS

The issues in this assembly can be reinforced in any lesson which requires the children to work or co-operate with each other, for example, playing a throw and catch game in PE or taking turns in a maths game.

RESOURCES AND ORGANIZATION

You will need: two children to be actors; a rope or two skipping ropes tied together – they should be just too short to reach across the assembly space; two bowls; two biscuits.

This assembly works well as a whole-school assembly with follow-up discussions in class groups. Sit the children in a semicircle so that they can see, but, for safety reasons, be away from the action.

WHAT TO DO

When the children are settled, talk to them about the work of a sheep-dog. What do they think a sheep-dog does? How important are they to the work of a sheep farmer? Explain that it is very important that a sheep-dog does exactly as he's told by the farmer, and if there are two dogs rounding up the sheep, they must work very well together.

Explain that you are going to tell them a story about two sheep-dogs who had to learn to work together so that they could do their job properly. Invite two children to help you tell the story. (Choose two children who will not solve the puzzle.)

Introduce the children as Rover and Patch.

Explain that Rover and Patch are two sheep-dogs who live on a farm. They are very important to the farmer because they help to round up the sheep. The only trouble was, the two dogs did not like each other and so the poor farmer never managed to get his sheep into the pen. Every time the dogs got near each other they snarled and growled at one another. They never managed to do the job properly because whenever one dog rounded up the sheep, the other one barked and the scared sheep would run off in the other direction. The poor farmer would despair and hold his head in his hands. It didn't matter what he did, the two dogs would not work together.

One day, the farmer decided to teach the dogs a lesson. At the end of a very busy day, when the dogs had spent a lot of time and energy not rounding up the sheep, the farmer took them back to the barn. Usually the two dogs would go off to their own corner and stare at each other all evening. This particular evening, however, the farmer got a long piece of rope which was not quite long enough to reach across the barn. He tied one end of the rope to Rover and the other end to Patch.

At this point, tie one end of the skipping rope around the waist of one child and the other end around the waist of the second child. Continue with the story.

The farmer got the dogs' suppers and put them into two dishes. He put one bowl in one corner of the barn and the other bowl in the opposite corner.

At this point, put one biscuit into each of the two bowls and place them at opposite sides of the assembly space. Encourage your two actors to act out the story while you continue with the tale.

The farmer shut the barn door and went inside for his supper. Rover and Patch sat down as far away from each other as they could. They sat and thought about what they were going to do. They were both very hungry after their busy day in the fields, but how were they going to reach their suppers? The rope wasn't quite long enough for them both to reach their bowls. Finally, they got up. Rover started pulling the rope one way to try to reach his bowl and Patch did the same.

Invite the two children to try to reach their biscuits at this point. Hold the rope to prevent over-enthusiastic pulling as they try to pull each other towards their own bowl. After a while, stop the action and invite the children to think of a way that they can both enjoy their suppers. Include the children watching in the discussion too. Someone may suggest that the two children must work together and share each other's supper if they are not to go without.

The two dogs did just that. First they shared Rover's supper and then Patch's.

Finish the story by saying that the dogs learned their lesson and that after that they always worked together, which meant that they managed to finish their job properly and in time.

Ask the children if there are any jobs in school which could be done quicker if two people worked together, for instance tidying the cloakroom or library. Are there times when someone asks for help and we say no? Spend a short time listing the jobs which can be done more quickly and easily if people work together, and invite the children to listen and think about their actions.

Finish the assembly with the following prayer:

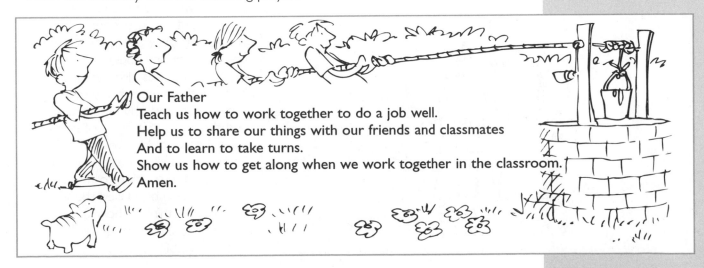

Our Father
Teach us how to work together to do a job well.
Help us to share our things with our friends and classmates
And to learn to take turns.
Show us how to get along when we work together in the classroom.
Amen.

Sing 'Hands to Work and Feet to Run' from *Someone's Singing, Lord* (A&C Black).

NOW OR LATER

■ Identify other occasions when the children must work together, for example playing snakes and ladders, or measuring how tall they are.
■ At the end of a practical activity in the classroom, gather the children together on the carpet area and share out the tidying-up jobs. List the children's names on a sheet of paper and write the job each child is responsible for alongside. When all the children have been allocated a job, start tidying up. Record the time it takes to do the whole job. You will need to stress the importance of returning to the carpet as soon as they have finished their job. Give the more able children responsibility for encouraging the other children to return quickly to the carpet area and work out how much time it took. Do they think the time can be improved?
■ Share the book *Bet You Can't* by Penny Dale (Walker Books) which shows the value of co-operation.
■ Talk to the children about Dragon Boat racing which could not take place without teamwork. This relates to the Chinese Festival celebrations. It is now celebrated by groups decorating long boats to resemble dragons. Races are held in several areas of Britain and the objective is to work in a team.

FEEDING TIME

OBJECTIVE
To learn that sometimes we must work together to solve problems.

CROSS-CURRICULAR LINKS

GEOGRAPHY
Talk about the countries that use chopsticks to eat their food. Look at a selection of oriental foods and discuss similarities and differences with traditional Western food.

RESOURCES AND ORGANIZATION
You will need: two long bean sticks and marshmallows.

It is very important that this activity is fully supervised and that an adult has hold of the 'chopsticks' at all times. The children watching must be supervised to keep them away from the participants.

This assembly is best delivered to the whole school, although it could equally be planned by a class to give to the rest of the school. Organize the children into a semicircle so that they can see the action clearly.

WHAT TO DO
Invite two children to come out to play the parts of a prince and princess. Begin the story thus:

Once upon a time, in a country far, far away there lived a beautiful princess. The princess was sad because her father, the king, said that she could not get married unless the person she chose could solve a problem he set him. What's more, he only had one chance to solve this problem.

Now the princess was in love with a prince who lived in the next country, but she knew her father would not agree to the marriage unless the prince could solve the problem. She was also worried because there were many men who came to try and solve the problem, and she knew that if any of them did solve it she would have to marry him. She watched all of them trying to work out the solution to the problem and after each one failed she tried and tried to think of how this problem could be solved herself. It was impossible.

The king however was a very clever person. He knew that the problem could only be solved in one way and that the person who solved it would be a very special person for his daughter to marry. This was the problem the king had set: the man who would be allowed to marry the princess had to eat a marshmallow with a pair of chopsticks. The chopsticks, however, were no ordinary chopsticks; they were two metres long!

At this point produce a marshmallow and the two bean sticks. Invite someone to come and use the 'chopsticks' to eat the marshmallow. Supervise the child closely, as the chopsticks will be very difficult to handle, and always make sure the children never put their mouths over the end of the beansticks. After several children have tried unsuccessfully to eat the marshmallow, ask if they can think of a way that the prince could eat the marshmallow with the sticks. If someone knows, invite them to demonstrate, supervising the activity closely. If not, continue with the story.

The prince was also very clever. He knew that the only way to eat the marshmallow was if he got someone to help. Guess who he chose? That's right, he chose the princess. He told her to hold the sticks in both hands and to carefully pick up the marshmallow. He then invited the princess to feed him the sweet.

At this point, invite the prince and princess to act out this part of the story. Ask the children to sit down when the prince has enjoyed his snack.

Spend some time thinking about the king. Do the children think he is happy or sad? Is he pleased that his daughter is getting married? Do they think the king will keep his promise?

Finish the story. Tell the children that the king was very pleased because he wanted his daughter to marry someone who understood that sometimes we have to work together to solve problems.

Sing the hymn 'Hands to Work and Feet to Run' from *Someone's Singing, Lord* (A&C Black) and say this prayer:

Dear Lord
Teach me to remember to help other people
when they ask for it.
Teach me to ask for help from others when I
need to so that we can all learn to work
together.
Amen.

SUGGESTIONS FOR DIFFERENTIATION

Talk about some of the problems that we need other people to solve for us. Perhaps when the television breaks down, or the car needs a service. Make a list of some of the people who solve problems for us such as a dentist, doctor, teacher, plumber. Ask the more able children to think of jobs which need more than one person to complete, for example building a house, making a window or performing surgery.

NOW OR LATER

■ Read the story of Jesus feeding the five thousand (Luke 9, verses 10–17) and talk about how the disciples worked together to give out the food to all the people.
■ Make a wall story about the journey of a letter to show the number of people who work together to make sure a letter is delivered.

The story of the Little Red Hen

Once upon a time there lived a Little Red Hen, her five little chicks, a pig, a dog and a cat. They all lived together on a farm and were the very best of friends.

One day the Little Red Hen decided to plant some seeds. She asked the pig, the dog and the cat for help.

'Who will help me plant these seeds?' she said.

'Not I,' said the pig.

'Not I,' said the dog.

'Not I,' said the cat.

'Then I will plant them myself,' she said. 'And my five little chicks will help me.'

The Little Red Hen and her chicks went into the field and planted the seeds.

Soon it was time to water the seeds, so the Little Red Hen went to the pig, the dog and the cat and asked for their help.

'Who will help me water the seeds?' she asked.

'Not I,' said the pig.

'Not I,' said the dog.

'Not I,' said the cat.

'Then I will water them myself,' said the Little Red Hen. 'And my five little chicks will help me.'

Continue the story in the same way for each of these actions:

Soon it was time to cut the corn.
Soon it was time to grind the corn into flour.
Soon it was time to bake a cake.

Continue with the story.

When the cake was cooked, the Little Red Hen went to the pig, the dog and the cat and said:

'Who will help me eat the cake?'

'I will,' said the pig.

'I will,' said the dog.

'I will,' said the cat.

What do you think the Little Red Hen said?

Listen to the children's suggestions before finishing the story.

'No you won't,' said the Little Red Hen. 'I will eat it myself, and my five little chicks will help me.'

Helping out

■ Write what the pig, the dog and the cat are thinking.

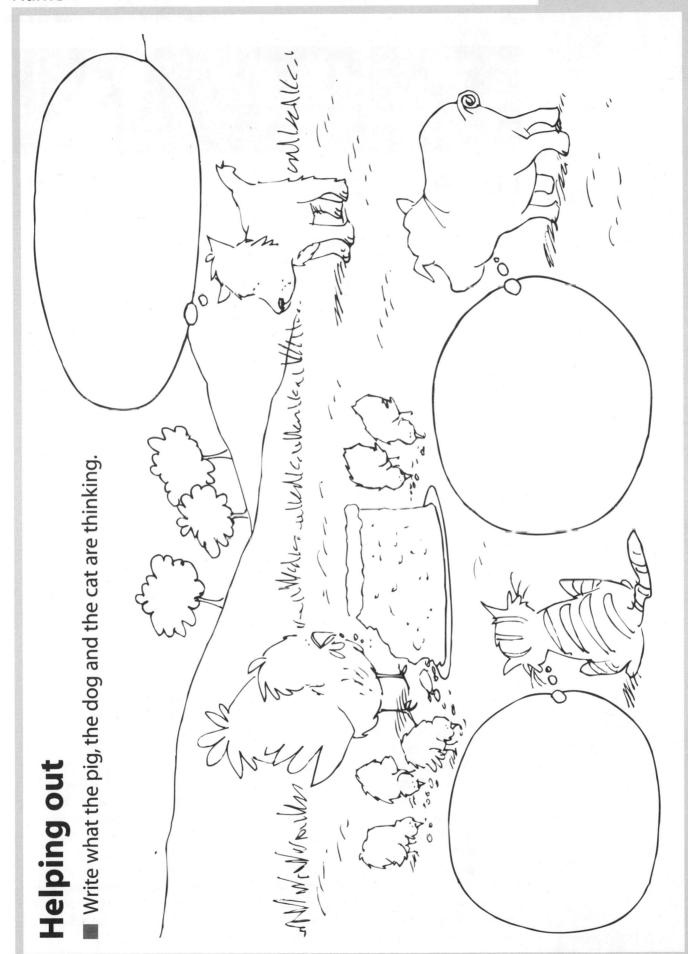

GETTING ALONG

The assemblies in this section focus on children learning to:
■ say sorry when they upset their friends
■ understand the need to share and take turns
■ begin to understand the need for rules of behaviour
■ understand the concept of temptation and how to overcome it.

MAKING RULES

OBJECTIVE
To help children to understand that we need to get along with each other when we are at school.

CROSS-CURRICULAR LINKS
PSHE
This assembly supports the PSHE programme of developing rules of conduct and allows the children to consider how they must behave to make the kind of school they want.

RESOURCES AND ORGANIZATION
You will need: a glove puppet and a container such as a bag or box in which to hide it; a large number of card or paper labels; a large display board or wall on which to pin the labels; drawing pins or adhesive tape; a dark felt-tipped pen. Make copies of photocopiable page 63, one for each child (for 'Now or later' activity).

This assembly can be conducted in one day or over two days. It is important that the whole school is involved if it is to be effective.

WHAT TO DO
When the children are settled, talk about the kind of things they like about school. What kind of games do they like to play at playtimes? Who do they like to play with?

Introduce the puppet to the children at this point. 'Talk' to the puppet and pretend that it is telling you about some unpleasant things that it experienced when it visited a park playground a long way from your school. Pretend that the puppet tells you

that when it tried to join in with a game of hide and seek, the children would not play with it. They didn't try to find it and it had to remain hidden until it got dark.

Ask the children what they thought of this treatment. Do they think this would have happened to the puppet in your school? Why not? Say that you would like to make this action into a rule. Write the rule on a label and attach it to the display board or wall. Make sure that you interpret the children's suggestions in a positive way. For example, if a child suggests that we should not ignore people who want to play, word it so that it reads something like 'Always let other people join in your games'.

Invite the puppet to tell you about other things it may be anxious about. Pretend to listen to it and repeat what it says. For example, you may say that it is worried about being called names. Ask the children whether this is something which they want to happen in their school. Hopefully they will answer 'No' so make this into a rule, again constructing it in a positive way, for example: 'Always call people by their proper names'. Attach it to the wall in the same way as before.

Continue until you have collected a number of rules for the children to consider. Read them to the children so that they are reminded of all the positive things they want to happen in their school. Give the children an opportunity to think about any other rules that they may want to include. Make sure that everyone's contribution is valued and valid. If you have any particular rules that you want to include or reinforce, use the puppet to help you do so.

You may wish to conclude the assembly at this point. If so, give the children time to reflect on the kind of school they want and the way each person must behave for this to happen. Finish with the hymn 'Peace Perfect Peace' from *Come and Praise* (BBC publications) and say a prayer, such as the one below.

If you wish to continue, tell the children that you now seem to have so many rules that you're worried they won't be able to remember them all. Explain that you want to keep all their excellent suggestions but combine them into five or six rules so that they are easier to remember.

Select a few rules from the board. Put these in a list and write one rule to represent all the ideas. For example, 'Keep yourself safe' could cover things such as walking in the school rather than running, always telling an adult where you are going, and so on. The rule 'Always be polite' could cover things like always listening to the person who is talking, remembering to say 'please' and 'thank you' and so on.

Bring the assembly to a close with a few moments of reflection outlined above. Read your five or six rules, sing the hymn and say the prayer.

> Dear Lord
> We want our school to be a place where everyone is happy,
> Where we can play together, be kind to each other and always remember to be sensible.
> We want our school to be a place where our things will be looked after,
> Where we will be safe and able to learn.
> Please help us to remember our school rules, which will make our school the place we want to be.
> Amen.

SUGGESTIONS FOR DIFFERENTIATION

Tell the older or more able children about the story of Moses and the Ten Commandments sent by God to tell people how to behave. These can often be seen displayed in a synagogue. Select for discussion those which you think the children will be able to understand.

NOW OR LATER

■ Give each child a copy of photocopiable page 63 for them to record the things that they are and are not allowed to do in school. The children should colour the green traffic light if the action is allowed and red if it is not. There are two blank squares on the sheet; you can either add two of your own school rules before photocopying it or ask the children to illustrate their own rules.

■ Talk to the children about classroom rules which may differ from school rules, such as taking turns to get the hall ready for assembly.

■ Talk about the rules that Muslims, Hindus and Sikhs follow. For example, Muslim children fast during Ramadan, Hindu children do not eat meat and Sikh boys keep their hair long and covered.

■ Talk about the Buddhist Eight-fold Path.

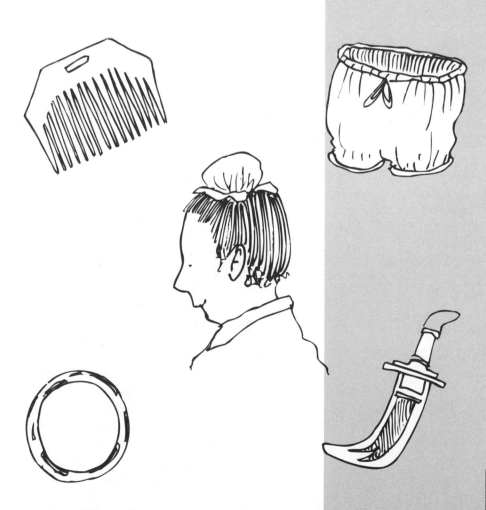

THE STORY OF JOSEPH AND HIS BROTHERS

OBJECTIVE

To begin to learn about forgiveness.

CROSS-CURRICULAR LINKS

The story of Joseph lends itself to: science and art with the investigation of colour; mathematics with the investigation of the number 12; English with the writing of one part of the story as a playscript, or looking up unfamiliar words such as 'famine' in a dictionary; and RE with the discussion of the characters' feelings in different parts of the story. There is also a suitable unit in the QCA design and technology scheme of work.

RESOURCES AND ORGANIZATION

It would be helpful to have a tape or CD of music from *Joseph and the Technicolor Dreamcoat* by Andrew Lloyd Webber and a CD/cassette player. The story of Joseph can be told over half a term and used as a starting point to discuss concepts of jealousy, anger, regret, sadness, joy and forgiveness.

The story is best acted out as a drama with the children having the opportunity to dress in appropriate costumes. For the purposes of this assembly, the story has been picked up towards the end, although it should be regarded as the last in a series of assemblies given to the whole school.

WHAT TO DO

Invite the children to recall the story so far. Remind them that Joseph's brothers have gone to Egypt to buy grain because of the famine and have met, but not recognized, their brother Joseph. Joseph, who is the governor of Egypt, has, however, recognized them and has given them grain and returned their silver. He has accused them of being spies and kept one of them in prison, telling them that they must return with their youngest brother to prove that they are not spies. Ask the children how Jacob felt about Benjamin going to Egypt. *Was he happy? Why was he concerned? Why did he eventually let him go?*

Continue with the story. When the brothers returned to Egypt with Benjamin, they immediately went to see Joseph. Joseph was overjoyed to see Benjamin and made an excuse to leave the room so that he could weep. Ask the children why this was.

Joseph told his steward to give his brothers sacks of grain and prepare them for the journey home. He told the steward to put as much food in each sack as the men could carry and place their silver in the mouth of the sack. He said 'Put my silver cup in the mouth of the sack belonging to Benjamin.'

The next day the brothers set off, but they had not gone far when Joseph's steward caught up with them. He told them that Joseph's silver drinking cup was missing from the palace.

Ask the children how they think the brothers felt at this time. Remind them that they still did not know that the governor was Joseph. *Do you think they were worried? They hadn't stolen anything and would not have known about the cup.*

Well of course, the steward searched the bags and found the missing cup in Benjamin's sack, so the brothers had to return to the palace. Joseph had said 'Whoever has the silver cup will become my slave while the rest of you may go free.'

The brothers begged Joseph to allow Benjamin to return home with them. They told him the story of how they had sold Jacob's other favourite son into slavery.

At this point, Joseph could not control himself any longer and revealed to his brothers who he was. He told them to go and tell his father that he was still alive and that he should come and live with him in Egypt. That is what they did, and Jacob came to Egypt to be reunited with Joseph.

Talk to the children about forgiveness. Ask them if they think Joseph had forgiven his brothers for selling him into slavery.

Play any track from *Joseph and the Technicolor Dreamcoat* while the children reflect on the ending to the story. Ask them to think of times when they have been unkind to a friend and had to ask for forgiveness. Are there occasions when they have forgiven a friend? Say 'The Lord's Prayer' together and finish the assembly by singing 'He's Got the Whole World in His Hands' from *Come and Praise* (BBC publications).

SUGGESTIONS FOR DIFFERENTIATION

Discuss some of the squabbles that the children may have had in the playground with their friends. Talk about how important it is to say sorry, forgive and make up.

Remind them that if they are the one being forgiven, it means making a promise not to repeat the action that caused distress in the first place.

NOW OR LATER
■ Read the story of Noah's Ark. Discuss why God sent a flood and the sign He sent to show that He had forgiven the people.
■ Talk to the children about Yom Kippur, when Jewish people confess and seek forgiveness.

TUSK, TUSK

RESOURCES AND ORGANIZATION

You will need a copy of the story *Tusk, Tusk* by David McKee (Beaver Books).

As long as the children are able to see the pictures in the story book, this can be a whole-school or class assembly.

WHAT TO DO

Gather the children together and talk to them about the differences between each other. Do they have the same colour hair, eyes, skin? Are they the same size, gender and shape? If you have already carried it out, remind them about the assembly entitled 'Don't judge a book by its cover' (page 60).

Begin reading *Tusk, Tusk* at this point, interspersing the text with questions at appropriate points. For example, ask the children why they think the elephants are fighting. Would they have been with the group of elephants that went into the jungle or would they have remained to fight? Use facial expressions to show the children which responses you like and ask them to give reasons for their choices.

Use the end of the story as an opportunity for reflection. Ask the children why they think the elephants with big ears were looking at the elephants with little ears. What do the children think is going to happen next in the story? Can they think of times when they have heard people commenting about someone because they look different? Reinforce the learning objective and the fact that we should not judge a person by the way he or she looks.

The hymn 'Peace Perfect Peace' from *Come and Praise* (BBC publications) is appropriate to support the learning objective. The words of the hymn 'Spirit of God', also from *Come and Praise*, make an appropriate prayer.

SUGGESTIONS FOR DIFFERENTIATION

Be aware of any children who may have had a problem recently and treat the introduction to the assembly with care and sensitivity. Try to include a personal story about the issues in the story to tell the children (but be aware of any sensitivities your pupils may have before choosing specific examples). This will encourage them to open up and add anecdotes from their own experiences and allow you to find out whether there are any issues within your school.

OBJECTIVE
To learn the importance of getting to know a person and not picking an argument just because he or she looks different.

CROSS-CURRICULAR LINKS
This assembly fits well in a programme of PSHE lessons which deals with issues such as bullying and racism. It can also be used as a starting point to discuss any issues, usually name calling, which may be present in the school.

NOW OR LATER

■ Tell the children the Bible story about Jesus healing the leper (Luke 5, verses 12–16).
■ The children could extend the story by writing another section about what happened between the elephants with big ears and the elephants with little ears.
■ With the children, create a picture book showing the different games they play together.

DON'T JUDGE A BOOK BY ITS COVER

OBJECTIVE

To begin to understand that you cannot get to know what a person is like just by the way he or she looks.

CROSS-CURRICULAR LINKS

SCIENCE

This activity can be developed into a 'feely' box activity to learn and understand about our senses.

You may like to link this assembly to the one entitled 'Who can we trust?' (page 22) which deals with having to get to know a person before we can usually trust them.

RESOURCES AND ORGANIZATION

You will need: three sets of objects wrapped in tissue paper and a table on which to display them at the front of the assembly. Set 1 should contain easily distinguishable objects such as a banana, a teapot or saucepan and a distinctive animal ornament. Set 2 should contain objects which are a little more difficult to guess and which perhaps can be guessed through shaking to see if the contents make a noise. Include objects such as a jigsaw in a rectangular box, an orange that will have a distinctive smell and a packet of biscuits. Set 3 should contain objects which are not easily guessed, for example, a ball which could be confused with an orange, a can of baked beans and a folded skipping rope.

This works best as a whole-school assembly.

WHAT TO DO

When the children are settled, talk to them about their particular or best friend. Why did they become friends? Was it because their parents are friends and they used to play together when they were younger? Do they have similar interests? Ask one or two children to talk about their particular friend. What kind of things do they do together?

Ask the children if they chose their friend because they had long hair, wore glasses or had bigger feet? Was it because they had blue eyes, brown skin or blond hair? Or did they choose their friend because they could play football, liked the same games or watched the same television programmes? Did the children become friends straight away or did they have to get to know each other first? Ask the children if they think it is possible to tell what a person is like just by looking at them, or do you have to get to know what a person is like inside? Explain that with some people it is easy to discover what they are like, but with other people it can take a lot of time and effort to really get to know them.

Tell the children that there is a saying, 'Don't judge a book by its cover'. Explain that you are going to play a game with them to show what this saying means.

At this point, place the first set of objects on the table for the children to see. Hold up the teapot or saucepan and invite the children to tell you what is inside the parcel. Repeat this with the other two objects. Ask the children if it was easy to guess what was wrapped in each parcel.

Now place the second set of objects on the table and explain that this set is more difficult to guess because they look similar to several objects. For each object, invite the children to say what it may be. When they have made a few suggestions, invite one child to feel, smell and shake the objects. Can he or she say what is inside the parcel now? Was it more difficult to guess what was wrapped in this set of parcels? Did the children have to 'get to know' the parcels before they could say for sure what they were? Explain that this is a bit like getting to know a person before you can say what they are like.

Place the objects in Set 3 on the table. Hold up the spherical shaped parcel and ask the children what may be inside. Invite one child to shake, squeeze and smell it. Is it easy to tell what is inside the parcel? Repeat the activity with the other objects. Why is it more difficult to guess what is inside this set of parcels?

Ask the children to think about the people they know. Can they tell what people are like just by looking at them? Are all people with blue eyes the same or do they have different characters and personalities? Should we like people because of the way that they look or should we get to know them first?

Talk to the children about how they get to know other people. What things do they do together? Talk about the importance of talking to each other, asking and answering questions, and talking about the things that they like to do.

Spend a few moments reflecting on how the children got to know one another. Think about the games they play in the playground, how they share the toys and equipment in activity sessions and work together in their groups in the classroom.

Say a short prayer about how important it is to get to know a person before deciding what they are like and sing an appropriate hymn such as 'Black and White' from *Someone's Singing, Lord* (A&C Black).

SUGGESTIONS FOR DIFFERENTIATION

Conduct the assembly in smaller class groups and, with additional adult support, use several sets of wrapped items. This will give every child an opportunity to consider the contents of at least one parcel in each set, and will focus reflection and reinforce the learning objective.

NOW OR LATER

■ Read the story of the Good Samaritan (Luke 10, verses 25–37) and discuss the issues.

■ Each day, place a different wrapped object in a designated place for the children to guess the contents. Make the object more difficult to guess as the week proceeds. Talk to the children about how easy or difficult it was to guess the content of the parcel.

■ Tell the Buddhist story of the King of the Birds and his daughter who chose a partner by his appearance but found that other qualities were needed; see *Buddhist Stories* by John Snelling (Wayland).

TEMPTATION

OBJECTIVE
To understand the meaning of temptation.

CROSS-CURRICULAR LINKS
ENGLISH
In drama, ask the children to invent their own television advert for advertising their favourite TV programme or holiday destination.

RESOURCES AND ORGANIZATION

This is effective as a whole-school assembly, although with some preparation it could be effective as a class assembly presented to the whole school.

WHAT TO DO

Introduce the assembly by explaining to the children that you are going to tell a story about a girl who gave in to temptation. Can any of the children explain what 'temptation' means?

Tell them a short story about a girl called Mary who was walking along the road to school when she saw a £10 note lying on the ground. *What would she do? Would she pick the note up and spend it at the shop later or would she give it to her teacher and explain where she had found it?* When Mary got to school, she went into her classroom and sat down for the register to be called. Her teacher, Mrs Brown, was late that morning and the headteacher was calling the register. She told the children that Mrs Brown had lost a £10 note on the way to school that morning and, as she

needed it to pay an important bill, had gone to get some more money. The headteacher asked the children if any of them had seen a £10 note on the way to school. *What did Mary do? Did she give in to the temptation to keep the money? Was she tempted to lie about finding the note? Would it be wrong to lie or not say anything? Would it be wrong to keep the money?*

Give the children a short time to think about what they would do if they found some money on the floor or pavement. Would they give in to the temptation to keep the money or would they try to find a way to return it? How then could they help others to overcome temptation? Talk about the other times the children may be tempted to do something wrong, for example being unkind to someone, or telling lies to prevent getting into trouble.

Say 'The Lord's Prayer' and sing 'He's Got the Whole World in His Hands' from *Come and Praise* (BBC publications) to finish the assembly.

SUGGESTIONS FOR DIFFERENTIATION

Back in the classroom invite a group of more able children to write and act out their own commercial or play with which to tempt their schoolmates. Invite the audience to say 'No' to temptation if it is wrong, or accept it if it is all right.

NOW OR LATER

■ Talk to the children about Lent. Have the children or someone they know given anything up for Lent?
■ Talk about healthy meals. Are the children's favourite foods healthy?
■ Tell the story of the time when Jesus went into the wilderness and was tempted by the devil. At the end of the story, ask the children if they think it was easy for Jesus to resist the temptation the devil offered. Why do they think this? Who did Jesus ask for help?
■ Tell the children about the Buddha's temptations during the 'enlightenment'. (During the time when the Buddha was looking for enlightenment, the demon, Mara, is reputed to have set many temptations to test him.)
■ Talk to the children about Ramadan. This is the month in which the Qur'an was revealed to the prophet Muhammad. It is spent in prayer and meditation. During this period, adult Muslims fast from dawn to dusk. They do not eat or drink. After sunset the fast is broken with a drink and something sweet such as a date. Young Muslims might fast for short periods.

Our school rules

Can we do these things in our school?

■ Colour green for yes.

■ Colour red for no.

■ Draw one thing that you are allowed to do in our school and one thing that you are not.

	Asking questions	Communicating	Reflecting	Evaluating	Empathizing	Explaining
Our wonderful world	✓		✓	✓		
All things bright and beautiful	✓	✓	✓			
Thank you for the world	✓	✓	✓			
A festival of light			✓	✓		
Let's celebrate		✓	✓	✓		
Friendship cake			✓		✓	✓
Thank you for my friends		✓		✓		
A circle of hands			✓	✓	✓	
Giving and receiving	✓		✓	✓		
Who can we trust?	✓		✓	✓		✓
Starting school	✓	✓	✓		✓	
We are all different, but we all have…	✓		✓		✓	✓
Lost and found			✓	✓		
Thank you for making me me		✓	✓			
I am special	✓	✓	✓			
I can do	✓	✓	✓			
The lost sheep			✓	✓		✓
Thinking for myself			✓	✓		✓
Helping out			✓		✓	✓
We all have a part to play			✓	✓	✓	✓
Learning to work together			✓	✓	✓	
Feeding time	✓	✓	✓	✓		
Making rules	✓		✓	✓		
The story of Joseph and his brothers			✓	✓		
Tusk, tusk			✓	✓	✓	
Don't judge a book by its cover			✓	✓	✓	
Temptation	✓		✓			✓